W...

Have you or a loved one been d...

Are you unsure about all the different heart problems there are?

Do you want to know how to avoid problems in the future?

Heart disease is very common and not only is it potentially disabling but it can also prove fatal.

This book explains:

- how the heart works
- what can go wrong and why
- worrying symptoms to be on the look out for
- very importantly how to keep your heart as healthy as possible.

Checking out troubling symptoms with your own GP is very important and this book is not intended to be a substitute for doing so.

For my amazing boys: Harry, Sam, and Archie.

First Steps to a Healthy Heart

Dr Simon Atkins

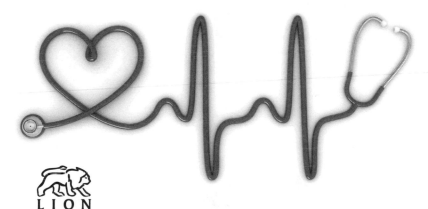

LION

Text copyright © 2019 Simon Atkins
This edition copyright © 2019 Lion Hudson IP Limited

Published by
Lion Hudson Limited
Wilkinson House, Jordan Hill Business Park
Banbury Road, Oxford OX2 8DR, England
www.lionhudson.com

ISBN 978 0 7459 8038 6
e-ISBN 978 0 7459 8085 0

First edition 2019

Acknowledgements
Diagrams pp.13, 39 © Sam Atkins.

A catalogue record for this book is available from the British Library

Printed and bound in the UK, August 2019, LH26

Contents

Introduction

On 15 April 1984, while performing on stage in front of a live television audience, the internationally renowned comedian and magician Tommy Cooper collapsed. As he slumped back into the curtain behind him the crowd laughed, thinking it was part of the act. But as the time ticked by and he remained motionless people began to realize that something was seriously wrong.

Cooper had not been play-acting at all; he'd in fact been having a massive heart attack as millions of TV viewers had looked on from their sofas. And despite the best efforts of paramedics he was pronounced dead on arrival at Westminster Hospital.

Tommy Cooper is not alone; other famous people, including *Carry On* actor Sid James and the American comedian and star of the film *The Producers*, Zero Mostel, have had what turned out to be fatal heart attacks while on stage. And other celebrities like David Bowie, US President Bill Clinton, Hollywood legend Elizabeth Taylor, and former England football manager Glen Hoddle have famously suffered from heart attacks too.

Heart disease is also likely to have affected at least one person that you know; either family or friends. In my own family I had two grandparents, my dad, and most recently my uncle who have all been affected.

But that's perhaps not surprising when you read the statistics that tell us how frighteningly common heart disease is. Research by the British Heart Foundation highlights some sobering figures for the UK alone. They have found that:

- there are around 7 million people currently living with heart disease
- each year there are 152,000 deaths from heart and circulatory diseases, 42,000 of which are premature, occurring in people under the age of seventy-five
- every three minutes someone is taken to hospital with a heart attack.

And globally, the World Health Organization estimates that every year 17.7 million people lose their lives as a direct result of heart disease. That's one third of all deaths on the planet each year. Heart disease is big business for the Grim Reaper.

But there is some good news alongside these frightening figures: treatments are getting better. We now have more drugs to help combat heart disease, operations are more successful with fewer complications, and we have more specialist cardiac units around the country where high-tech, life-saving treatment can be administered within minutes of your arrival by ambulance.

So whereas in the 1960s seven out of ten people who had a heart attack in Britain would die as a direct result, that statistic has been flipped on its head and in the twenty-first century seven out of ten people now survive.

The even better news is that there is plenty that each of us can do to look after our heart to try to avoid becoming one of these statistics at all. And that's where this book comes in.

Over the next ten chapters we'll take a look at the structure and function of the heart when all is well, before looking in detail at some of the problems that can develop, or you can be born with. These include high blood pressure, disease of your heart's valves or its electrical system, and disorders of the heart muscle itself. We'll also look at the most frightening symptom of heart trouble: chest pain.

We'll be focusing not only on the causes of heart trouble, but also on how they can be detected and the treatments that are available to help put them right. There's also a chapter about how you can enjoy a good quality of life even if you do develop heart disease, which covers coping at work, the nitty gritty of having safe and enjoyable holidays, and how to maintain a happy and satisfying sex life.

And perhaps most importantly, there's a chapter on the key lifestyle changes you can make to try to avoid the ravages of heart disease altogether. Spoiler alert: it'll involve exercise, a healthy diet, and quitting cigarettes.

But if you're up for it, do read on.

We begin the quest for a healthy heart by looking at the structure of the organ itself and at how it continues to beat – day in, day out – to keep us alive.

1
How your heart works

I'm writing this chapter in early February and with Valentine's Day fast approaching the shops are currently stocked full of cards and balloons emblazoned with images of hearts. But these love hearts don't even bear a passing resemblance to the actual shape and structure of the fist-sized muscular organ pumping away inside our chest, even when it's love and romance that's making it pump that little bit faster.

In this chapter we will consider what the heart actually looks like, the electrical system that repeatedly fires it into action, and the way in which it supplies its own muscle with the blood that allows it to pump the rest of the blood around our bodies 100,000 times per day.

What does the heart do?

The heart is, in essence, a pump. Its job is to ensure that blood can circulate all around the body so that it can supply our brain, muscles, and other vital organs with the oxygen and nutrients they need to keep working and keep us alive.

All of the oxygen that we need is breathed in through our lungs where it is then absorbed into the bloodstream. The nutrients enter our bodies through our mouths as the food we eat and drinks we swallow, and once the contents of our meals and snacks have been broken down into their constituent proteins, fats, carbohydrates, vitamins, and minerals in our gut they, like the oxygen, are absorbed into our bloodstream where they can then be propelled by our hearts to all corners of our bodies.

In short, if the heart stops pumping, then we stop too.

Where is your heart?

The heart is situated pretty much in the middle of your chest, sandwiched between your left and right lungs. Most of it lies directly behind your breastbone but its apex at the bottom is under your sixth rib on the left hand side.

A small number of people (thought to be around one in 12,000 of us) are born with the heart the other way around, as a mirror image of its position in everyone else. This is known as dextrocardia, from the Latin word *dexter*, which means "right". People with dextrocardia don't tend to run into any serious medical problems but they have provided endless opportunities for doctors to fool young medical students, because they can't hear a heartbeat when the usual left-hand side of their chest is listened to and their chest X-rays always look back to front.

The structure of the heart and circulation

The heart is at the centre of a complex system of blood vessels whose job it is to carry the oxygen-rich blood from the lungs throughout the body and back again so the process can be repeated over and over, 24/7, until the moment we die. It's reckoned that each day 23,000 litres of blood are pumped around this system.

Blood flow through the heart

The heart is essentially made up of four chambers: the left and right atria and the left and right ventricles (see Fig.1 opposite). Blood that has been around the body and been stripped of its oxygen returns to the right atrium in one of two large veins, either the superior or the inferior vena cava. The inferior vena cava also contains the nutrients that have been absorbed from the gut.

From the right atrium, the blood then passes into the right ventricle before being pumped through one of two large blood vessels called the pulmonary arteries back to the lungs where it can pick up a fresh supply of oxygen.

Once oxygenated it passes back to the left atrium of the heart in the pulmonary veins. From the left atrium it then heads into the left ventricle, the heart's main pumping chamber, which then contracts to push it through another large blood vessel called the aorta from where it flows off around the body once more.

Heart valves

In order to stop the blood flowing backwards into the chambers it has already passed through, there are four valves which are designed to shut tight once the chamber has been emptied. These valves sit between the atria and ventricles on each side and between the ventricles and the pulmonary artery and aorta.

These valves are called:
- tricuspid valve (because it has three flaps) – between the right atrium and right ventricle
- pulmonary valve – between the right ventricle and pulmonary artery
- bicuspid valve (because it has two flaps) or mitral valve (because it looks like a bishop's mitre) – between the left atrium and left ventricle

• aortic valve – between the left ventricle and aorta.

The tricuspid and mitral valves are prevented from turning inside out when the heart contracts by the chordae tendineae, which anchor them to the walls of their respective ventricles via small muscles called papillary muscles. These contract to keep the chordae under tension. Often called "heart strings" because of their appearance inside the heart, the chordae tendineae are really more like the guy ropes on a tent, or rigging on a ship's sail.

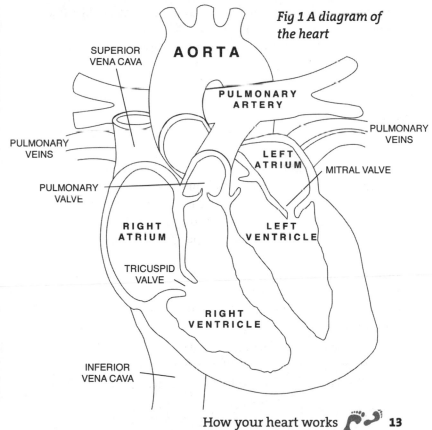

Fig 1 A diagram of the heart

SUPERIOR VENA CAVA

AORTA

PULMONARY ARTERY

PULMONARY VEINS

PULMONARY VEINS

LEFT ATRIUM

MITRAL VALVE

PULMONARY VALVE

RIGHT ATRIUM

LEFT VENTRICLE

TRICUSPID VALVE

RIGHT VENTRICLE

INFERIOR VENA CAVA

Blood vessels: the arteries and veins

All blood vessels that leave the heart are called arteries, while those that bring the blood back are all called veins. Arteries have muscular walls which can make the diameter of these vessels wider or narrower and so change the pressure under which the blood is being pumped. This is what we call our blood pressure (more of which in Chapter 8) and it helps make sure the blood reaches the tips of our fingers and toes.

Veins, on the other hand, aren't as muscular and they depend on the squeezing of muscles in our legs to help push blood back towards the heart. They have a number of small, bicuspid, valves inside them to stop blood moving in the wrong direction and going back to where it came from. For example, the femoral vein, which runs the length of the thigh, has around six of these valves.

The arteries and veins in our bodies form an interconnected network of vessels, much like branches on a tree. Blood passes along the equivalent of the tree's main trunk (the aorta) and then into large branches, then smaller ones, and finally into the twigs at the ends of those branches. In our body these vessels are called arteries, arterioles, and capillaries as they decrease in size. The capillaries then pass the blood into small veins (venules), and then on into increasingly larger veins until the blood arrives back at the heart.

How the heart pumps

Much like the pump in a home central heating system or the fuel pump in a car engine, the pump in your chest is sparked into life by our very own electrical ignition system. Thankfully, we don't have to remember to turn a key or flick a switch to get this one going. In fact, it all happens automatically without even involving our brains. Which is perhaps just as well because if we had to think our hearts into action, we might well forget when we were distracted and a heart-stopping moment in a film or TV show might actually do just that.

The pacemaker

The trigger for the heart's electrical activity, which goes on to produce each of our heartbeats, is called the sinoatrial node (SA node). It gets its name because of its position at the top of the right atrium next to what's called the sinus venosus, where the superior vena cava enters the heart.

The SA node was first discovered in the early 1900s by a medical student, Martin Flack, who was studying the heart of a mole. It consists of a dense collection of specialized heart muscle cells that repeatedly generate electrical charge which, they then discharge seventy to eighty times per minute.

The conducting system

Once produced in the SA node the charge quickly spreads through both atria causing the muscles in their walls to contract and pump the blood into the ventricles. Next the electrical impulse reaches the atrioventricular or AV node.

This node, like the SA node, is another collection of specialized muscle cells, situated in the middle of the heart between the atria and ventricles. Its job is to slow down and regulate the electrical signal that has come from the atria to ensure that they have completely emptied their blood into the ventricles and that the heart doesn't beat too fast.

Next the charge passes into a bundle of electrical fibres, called the bundle of His (named after the Swiss doctor, Wilhelm His, who first discovered them in 1893), as it is transmitted from the atria to the ventricles. It then follows one of two pathways, through either the left or right bundle of fibres, to stimulate the left and right ventricles to contract from the bottom up and squeeze their blood on to the next stage of its journey.

Once the ventricles have contracted, the electrical signal in them is reset and their muscles relax and another wave of charge heads out of the SA node to repeat the whole process all over again. And all of this takes place in generally less than a second.

Mythbuster

Heart failure happens when your heart stops beating.

Heart failure is the term used to describe what happens when the heart stops pumping as well as it should. This is most commonly caused by damage to the heart muscle, for example after a heart attack, or because of disease or damage to the heart valves meaning the blood does not flow through the heart and out into the circulatory system as efficiently as it should.

It can also be caused by conditions which slow down the heartbeat, but if the heart stops beating altogether it results in what's called a cardiac arrest, which can be fatal in just a matter of minutes.

2
Common symptoms

In this chapter we will take a brief look at some of the most common symptoms you might experience that should ring alarm bells that you may have a problem with your heart. They can, of course, be caused by other problems, but any of these should trigger you to make an appointment with your GP to find out what's going on.

The four most frequent symptoms – the headline acts of heart disease – are:

- chest pain
- shortness of breath
- palpitations
- ankle swelling.

Chest pain

As we'll see in much more detail in Chapter 4, chest pain can be caused by a variety of different underlying medical conditions and can have a range of qualities to it, from being a stabbing pain, to feeling as though you've got a rather large elephant sitting down on your breastbone. But however you experience it, and whatever the cause turns out to be, getting regular bouts of severe chest pain is not a good symptom to ignore.

In general, pain related to the heart occurs in the middle of the chest and is frequently brought on by pretty much any type of exertion, from a brisk walk to using your vacuum cleaner.

It can be mild or severe and won't necessarily conform to the medical textbook (or NHS website) description of being a heaviness. In fact, descriptions of pain that has turned out to be due to heart disease include:

- tightness
- fullness
- squeezing
- heavy pressure
- crushing
- like heartburn or indigestion.

So the bottom line here is to seek medical advice if you get any of these types of chest pain, or if you get any others I've not listed that are worrying you. And don't be put off getting in touch because you think you're too young, in good physical shape, you don't like to bother people, or have too busy a lifestyle to make an appointment. I've seen very active, thin, young people have heart attacks and many people who've regretted not seeing a doctor sooner than they did.

Shortness of breath

We've all, no doubt, felt out of breath when we've done a bit more exercise than we're used to, or when we're unfit. It can also be a symptom of a heavy cold, smoking, being overweight, or a panic attack.

But regular breathless episodes with a minimal amount of

exertion, or nothing to explain them, need checking out.

Breathlessness related to the heart can be caused by:

- a heart attack
- heart failure
- palpitations
- heart valve disease.

We'll be looking at these in more detail in subsequent chapters but the take-home message for now is that you should certainly see your doctor:

- if it's lasted more than a month
- if it's brought on by minimal exercise
- if you get pain with it
- if you feel your heart racing at the same time and you've not been exercising
- if it happens when you lie down
- if you get ankle swelling with it
- if it worries you for any other reason whatsoever!

Palpitations

Palpitations are the sensation you get when your heart is beating really quickly, fluttering, or beating irregularly. They are not a disease in themselves but a symptom of something potentially abnormal going on with your heart.

Thankfully, they are often harmless and more annoying than serious. And they can be set off by a whole range of different triggers.

Non-cardiac (heart-related) triggers
These can include:

- exercise
- caffeine in coffee and tea

- alcohol
- lack of sleep
- being stressed or anxious
- medication such as asthma inhalers, antidepressants, and some antibiotics (especially erythromycin and clarithromycin)
- hormone changes such as during periods and the menopause and because of an overactive thyroid gland
- anaemia
- fever
- dehydration.

Cardiac causes
These can include:
- electrical problems called arrhythmias (like atrial fibrillation and supraventricular tachycardia)
- valve disease
- muscle abnormalities (cardiomyopathies)
- heart failure.

We'll be looking in more detail at these cardiac causes in later chapters of the book, but they are the reason you need to take palpitations seriously and you should see your GP if they last a long time, they are associated with other symptoms like chest pain, breathlessness or giddiness, or you're simply bothered about why they're happening.

Ankle swelling
As you'll no doubt have guessed, swelling of your ankles and feet doesn't necessarily mean you've got heart trouble, but it can do. So as with the symptoms above, it's worth taking note of.

Once again we can look at the causes in terms of being either cardiac or non-cardiac. And as you'll see, many of the non-cardiac causes are in no way even vaguely serious.

Non-cardiac causes
These include:
- standing up too long
- sitting down too long
- a flight on an aeroplane or a long car or coach journey as a passenger
- hot weather
- being overweight
- having varicose veins
- an ankle sprain
- arthritis of the joint, or gout
- liver or kidney disease.

Cardiac causes
- Heart failure.
- Side effects of blood pressure medicines (calcium channel blockers).

We'll be looking at the causes of heart failure in later chapters, but even though it's only one among many other potentially less serious causes, if you have recurrently swollen ankles you should certainly get it checked out, particularly if it's associated with shortness of breath or you're known to already have a type of heart disease.

Heart disease is a man's problem.

Sorry ladies, but the statistics actually tell us that more women than men die of heart disease each year. In fact, it is the leading cause of death in women, whereas it comes second to cancer in men.

3
Checking out your heart

If you've experienced any of the symptoms mentioned in the previous chapter, or you're just concerned that some other symptom you've noticed might be heart related, where do you go to find out what's what? And how urgently?

In this chapter we'll look at the available options for having your heart checked so that either your condition can be treated or your mind can be put at rest. But it's important to remember that some of the symptoms in Chapter 2 are not just early warning signals that something's wrong and needs looking into; they can be multi-decibel alarm bells telling you to take action now. So while it may be alright to wait for the next routine appointment at your GP surgery with some symptoms, others are potentially life threatening and warrant picking up the phone and dialling 999 immediately.

My grandpa, a stiff upper-lipped, no nonsense Geordie who had served on HMS *Belfast* in the Arctic convoys in World War Two, put his crushing central chest pain while driving back to Portsmouth from a holiday in Cornwall down to a touch of indigestion, even though the antacids he took didn't remotely take the edge off his symptoms. He managed to get home and had an early night (and no doubt a medicinal cup of tea) to see if he would feel better the next morning. But when he woke, the pain was as intense as ever and he eventually gave up on the heartburn remedies and took himself to hospital.

Once in the emergency department he was wired up to an ECG machine (more of which later in the chapter) and it very quickly became apparent that he'd been having a massive heart attack while he'd motored up the A303 the day before. He mercifully survived the episode, but having left it so long to seek medical attention, the damage that his heart had sustained over the previous twenty-four hours was sadly permanent.

And he's by no means alone. Many of my own patients have either not quite taken their symptoms as seriously as they should do, stuck their heads in the sand and ignored them, mistaken them for symptoms of something else, or unnecessarily gritted their teeth so as not to bother the doctor.

If you have symptoms that could be caused by a problem with your heart it's not just OK to bother the doctor with them – it's imperative that you do. Or tragically they may be the last symptoms you ever ignore.

Emergency symptoms

These are symptoms you should never ignore and should have you reaching for the phone and dialling 999 immediately. Please don't ring your doctor's surgery as this might delay you getting life-saving treatment.

Symptoms of a heart attack

- Chest pain: usually in the centre or left side of the chest and most often felt as a heavy, crushing, or tightening sensation.
- Pain in other parts of your body. People most commonly

 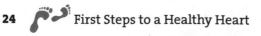

experience pain in the neck, jaw, and left arm but it can also be felt in the upper abdomen and back.
- Feeling faint.
- Shortness of breath.
- Feeling sweaty and clammy.
- Nausea and vomiting.
- Anxiety.
- Coughing or wheezing.

You don't have to have a full set of these symptoms to be having a heart attack, so if you have some but feel generally dreadful you need to call 999 immediately and leave the experts to find out exactly what's going on.

Symptoms of a severe arrhythmia
These are the kinds of symptoms you might experience if your heart starts beating erratically:
- a fluttering in your chest, or palpitations (sensation of the heart beating really quickly)
- a slow heartbeat
- shortness of breath
- chest pain
- light-headedness or giddiness
- fainting, or strong feeling that you're going to faint.

Again, if these are severe and you're struggling for breath or have severe chest pain that isn't settling, or you've fainted, you should seek emergency help by calling 999.

Routine symptoms
If your symptoms don't tick any of the boxes above, but you're getting such frequent bouts of them that they are starting to

become troublesome, then you should book an appointment with your GP.

And you can also book in for a check-up if you have a family history of heart disease and wonder what you can do to avoid developing it yourself, or have no symptoms or family history but have been frightened out of your wits by a newspaper or magazine article about heart problems and need some sensible, evidence-based information and reassurance.

At the doctors' surgery

When you book for a heart check-up you may be offered an appointment with a GP or with a highly qualified nurse called an advanced nurse practitioner (ANP). Rest assured either will be able to begin your assessment safely and effectively, and if you're booked to see a nurse you're likely to be given a longer appointment to begin to go through your concerns.

Medical history

Whoever you see, the first thing they'll do is ask you about your symptoms. They'll need to assess:

- the exact nature of your symptoms
- how long ago you started to notice them
- what brings them on
- how long they last
- what makes them worse
- what might make them better (such as stopping what you're doing)
- whether they are becoming more severe or more frequent
- whether you've had them before.

They'll also want to find out about any family history in near relatives, of heart trouble and some information about your risk factors for heart problems, such as whether you smoke, whether you have a good diet, and whether you have a sedentary or active lifestyle.

Once they have a clear idea of what's been going on, you'll get a physical examination.

The examination

The examination will be aimed at assessing not only your heart and circulation, but also your general physical condition, as this has a bearing on your heart's health too.

So, first of all, the doctor or ANP will take a look at you as this can provide some really useful information before they've even laid a hand on you or picked up a stethoscope.

Sir Arthur Conan Doyle, the inventor of Sherlock Holmes, was a Scottish doctor and he used the observational skills he'd learned as a medical student as the basis for the great detective's deductive powers. And while you won't be assessed to see whether you're a master criminal, you will be checked for signs that might point towards a cause for your symptoms.

These might include the pale skin of anaemia, blueness of lips if you're short of breath, your weight, your level of mobility as you enter the room or walk down the corridor, and the tell-tale staining of nicotine on your fingers that identifies you as a smoker.

Next comes the hands-on stuff. You will have checks of pulse and blood pressure and maybe have a probe popped onto a finger to check your oxygen levels. Your heart will be listened to with a stethoscope to check its rate and rhythm, and for murmurs (whooshing sounds that suggest your valves aren't working properly).

Other checks may well include a look at your neck, where a pulsating jugular vein can be a sign of heart failure, palpation of foot and leg pulses, a look at your ankles for swelling, a listen to your chest with the stethoscope, and measurements of height and weight.

Simple tests

Once the doctor or nurse has completed the history and examination they are likely to have a much clearer idea of what's going on and so will discuss the next steps with you. If they are concerned that your condition is serious, then this may involve a referral to hospital sooner rather than later. But, in the main, they are likely to suggest a variety of simple tests to fine-tune their diagnosis and to check your cardiovascular system in more detail.

Blood and urine tests
- Blood tests: checking your blood count, blood sugar, kidney function, liver function, and blood lipid levels (which include a cholesterol test). Other more detailed blood tests might be used if you have symptoms of heart failure.
- Urine dipstick: kidney problems can cause high blood pressure so you'll be checked for these.

Electrocardiogram (ECG)
An ECG, often called a "heart tracing", is a simple test which will often be carried out at your doctor's surgery. It's a test that looks at the electrical activity of your heart.

The test involves having twelve sensors stuck to bare skin on your chest, arms, and legs which are connected by wires to the ECG recording machine. The test only takes a few minutes and will allow your doctor to check for some specific, abnormal patterns in your heart's electrical activity which can help them diagnose certain causes of chest pain, arrhythmias, and cardiomyopathies (heart muscle abnormalities).

Chest X-ray

In addition to these tests in your doctor's clinic or surgery, you may be asked to go to a local hospital for a chest X-ray. This can be particularly helpful if your doctor is looking for signs of heart failure.

X-rays are a type of invisible radiation that passes through your body. The energy from this radiation is absorbed at different rates by our body tissues, and a detector on the other side of your body picks up the rays so that a black and white image can be generated.

Areas of the body that are full of air, like lungs, pick up less radiation and appear black in the eventual image, whereas the heart, a thicker tissue, picks up more of the rays and so shows up white.

The procedure is completely painless and takes a few minutes to perform.

More detailed tests

Once the simple tests have been completed, your family doctor may advise that you need some more detailed tests carried out either to fine-tune your diagnosis further, or to help assess treatment options. All of these will be carried out in hospital and are likely to involve a referral to a heart specialist (cardiologist).

The tests below are the ones that are most commonly carried out, but the list isn't exhaustive and cardiologists have a few other, more specialized, tests up their sleeves that are beyond the scope of a "First Steps" book.

Ambulatory ECG

This works in the same way as the ECG mentioned earlier in the chapter but this time the electrodes will be wired up to a small portable recorder that you will wear for the next twenty-four to forty-eight hours. This recorder will then be able to pick up the electrical activity of your heart day and night as you go about your normal activities. You can't wear it in the shower or bath though because water and electrical devices don't mix very well!

Most recorders have some sort of button to press when you experience symptoms (such as palpitations or breathlessness) so that when the trace is analysed the electrical activity recorded can be correlated with your symptoms to see what's going on.

Stress ECG

This test takes ECG recordings while you walk on a treadmill, allowing doctors to assess whether chest pain is coming from your heart. There are certain ECG patterns that suggest the heart is under strain and these can be picked up while you exert yourself on the treadmill.

This used to be the first-line test for assessing chest pain but it has been superseded by other tests such as stress echocardiograms and myocardial perfusion scans, which we'll look at below. Its main weakness is that it's not suitable for people with mobility or breathing issues, who are very often not able to complete the tests and therefore won't have any meaningful results.

Echocardiogram

This test is carried out with ultrasound equipment similar to that used in antenatal clinics to check the health of growing babies inside pregnant mums.

Most commonly the scan is carried out using a probe on the

 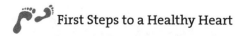

outside of your chest, but in some cases, where a more detailed look at the heart is needed, it can be done under sedation, using a special probe that goes down your oesophagus (gullet).

When used in these ways, the scan shows the structure of the heart, how well it's pumping, and the structure and function of the heart's four valves.

It can also be used for the stress echocardiogram test mentioned above. In this case the scan is performed while your heart is under stress and pumping faster. This is triggered either by exercise (on a treadmill or exercise bike), or with drugs administered at the time of the test.

A stress echocardiogram is useful to assess whether heart function is affected by narrowing of your arteries (atherosclerosis).

Angiogram

An angiogram uses a thin tube, called a catheter, to put a special dye into the blood vessels around your heart to check for narrowing or blockages. It is done in hospital in a catheter lab using either X-rays to show up the dye in the blood vessels or a CT scanner (a more sophisticated X-ray machine shaped like a doughnut).

Depending on the technique being used, the catheter will be put into either a vein in your arm or an artery in your groin. It's then threaded through your circulatory system until it reaches your heart.

Electrophysiological studies

These tests also involve catheters but this time they are used to analyse the heart's electrical system to look for, and sometimes treat, conduction problems.

The catheter is usually inserted into the groin and then passed up to the heart where it can pick up and be used to destroy abnormal electrical pathways. The test is usually carried out under sedation and can take between two and three hours.

Myocardial perfusion scans

This is a much fancier version of the older stress ECG. This time, instead of watching for changes in an ECG reading to show problems with blood flow to the heart, specialists inject a radioactive tracer substance into a vein, which can then be detected by a special camera as it flows around your circulation system and into your heart muscle.

The test is carried out both at rest and with your heart under stress (where you'll again either exercise on a bike or treadmill, or be given an injection of a drug). This will help doctors see which areas of your heart have a good blood supply and which ones don't and are therefore likely to have blocked or narrowed arteries.

4
Chest pain

For most of us, when we think about heart trouble the first symptom that tends to spring to mind is chest pain. So much so that people will often come to see me in my surgery with a variety of different types of pain in their chests, worried that their heart is about to give out on them at any moment, perhaps even during the course of our consultation. If that were to happen it would be dreadful enough, but to think that mine would be the last face they saw before they succumbed has got to be truly devastating.

Thankfully, for the vast majority (and I'm talking 99.99 per cent here[1]), the consultation passes without any life-threatening event and they make it home safely. And even the remaining 0.01 per cent, who may have genuinely experienced cardiac chest pain, have all, so far, made it to hospital or for further investigation safely.

The last time I was confronted with a genuine heart attack it came not from one of my own patients but when a builder

---

1   These statistics are not based on accurate research, but I wanted to underline how exceedingly rare such events are!

working up the road from the health centre wandered in to reception because he had had severe chest pain all morning and thought he'd better get it looked at in his lunch break (the surgery was conveniently situated between the house he was working on and the local bakery, so he made a fortuitous detour).

The staff reacted quickly and although I was initially a bit grumpy at having been interrupted while scoffing my own sandwich, our team's efforts resulted in a virtually instantaneous ECG in our treatment room, which showed immediately that his heart was the cause of his pain. Thanks to a swift response to our 999 call, in just a further twenty minutes he was being packed off in the back of an ambulance having been given a dose of aspirin and a whiff of oxygen while he waited.

And thankfully he survived to tell the tale, and very kindly came back a couple of weeks later to thank us for our help.

In this chapter we will look at how you can tell if your chest pain is simple and straightforward, due to something other than your heart, or in the league of our builder mentioned above. We'll begin by looking at what sort of problems can cause pains in the chest and the types of pains they can cause.

The causes of chest pain

Although for many of us the heart is the most famous and most worrying cause of chest pain, other organs and bodily structures in the chest can cause similarly severe pain – some, but by no means all, with similarly serious consequences. These are:

- lungs
- chest wall
- digestive system.

While we're only really focusing on heart problems in this book, we will have a quick look at the way each of these three can

 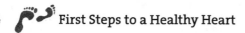

produce chest pain and the subtle differences between them
that help medical staff sort out which is which.

Lungs

Condition	What is it?	What are the symptoms?
Pulmonary embolism	A blood clot on the lungs which cuts off blood supply to part of the lung tissue.	Sudden, sharp pain that may worsen with deep breaths. Usually associated with shortness of breath.
Pneumothorax	This is when air builds up between the inside of the rib cage and the lung, causing the lung to collapse.	Sudden, sharp, stabbing pain on one side of the chest. Once again it can be accompanied by breathlessness.
Pleurisy	Inflammation of the pleura, the tissue that covers the outside of the lungs.	Sharp pain on taking a deep breath. The pain might also go up to the tips of the shoulders. It is generally caused by an infection so may be accompanied by a cough and fever.

Chest wall

Condition	What is it?	What are the symptoms?
Costochondritis	The cartilage between the ribs and the breastbone becomes inflamed.	Both sharp and dull pain in the chest wall. Can be worse on taking a deep breath, certain movements, or pressure on the chest wall.
Muscle pain	Pain in muscles because of overuse or conditions like fibromyalgia.	Pain can be on either or both sides of the chest. There are tender areas when pressed and it gets worse with certain movements.
Bruised ribs	The result of an injury to the ribs, for example after a fall or playing sport.	Ribs may be tender and the pain gets worse after a deep breath.

Digestive system

Condition	What is it?	What are the symptoms?
Gastritis	Inflammation of the stomach which is usually experienced as indigestion.	Gnawing or burning pain between meals and/or at night.
Reflux	When acid from the stomach moves up the oesophagus (gullet) into the throat.	Burning pain behind the breastbone. Often accompanied by an acidic taste in the mouth.

Gallstones	Small stones that form in the gallbladder which can cause pain as they are passed.	Spasmodic, colicky pain felt in the right upper abdomen which can often spread to the chest. Usually triggered by eating fatty meals.

While knowing about these different causes of chest pain may be reassuring, this is not intended as a guide to self-diagnosis. So if you have chest pain, of whatever kind, you should still see a doctor and if it's severe, call an ambulance.

We now move on to look at heart-related chest pains that are caused by either angina or, most seriously, a heart attack.

Angina

Angina (or to give it its full title, angina pectoris) is the term used to describe episodes of severe discomfort, or full-on pain, which most commonly begin in the centre of the chest and may then spread to the neck, the jaw, and down the left arm. Many people describe it as tightness around the chest and it is often associated with a feeling of shortness of breath. It is most commonly brought on by some form of exertion, which needn't be full-on sporting exercise but can be something like a brisk walk, rushing up the stairs, or running for a bus. It tends to settle with rest after around ten minutes.

Who gets angina?

Angina is a common problem, with around 20,000 people in the UK and an estimated 500,000 people in the United States developing it each year. It's more common in people over the age of fifty and occurs in men more than women.

There are a number of risk factors that increase your chances of developing it, especially if you have more than one of them. These include:

- smoking or chewing tobacco
- diabetes
- high blood pressure
- obesity
- family history of heart disease
- lack of exercise.

What causes the chest pain?

All the muscles in our bodies need a good blood supply to provide them with the fuel (glucose) and oxygen they need to produce the energy they require to work effectively. Heart muscle is no exception and so one of the first places oxygenated blood heads for when it is pumped out of the heart through the aorta is the heart muscle itself, which receives its blood supply via the coronary arteries.

If the oxygen supply is insufficient then pain will develop, much as it does in our leg muscles when we have to push ourselves to run up a hill. The more we exert ourselves, the more oxygen and fuel is needed, which is why pain tends to develop during exercise rather than at rest.

The reduction of blood flow to heart muscle is brought about by the development of what is called atherosclerosis within the coronary arteries. This is the result of plaques of cholesterol, fat, and smooth muscle cells building up in the walls of these arteries. The plaques lead to narrowing of the blood vessels and they reduce the elasticity of the vessel walls, which together result in the reduced blood flow to the muscles (see Fig. 2 opposite).

Fig. 2 Development of atherosclerosis

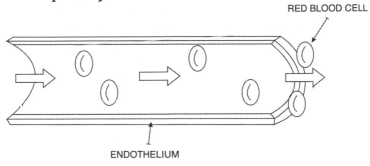

RED BLOOD CELL

ENDOTHELIUM

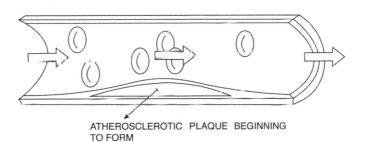

ATHEROSCLEROTIC PLAQUE BEGINNING
TO FORM

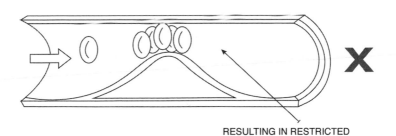

RESULTING IN RESTRICTED
BLOOD FLOW

How is it diagnosed?

If you develop chest pains like these then you need to see a doctor. They will not just "go away" as some of my patients have mistakenly thought. If they are severe they need to be taken extremely seriously and you should dial 999 and get yourself assessed at your nearest emergency department.

The baseline tests that will be carried out will include:

- blood tests (see Chapter 3 for more detail about these)
- an ECG
- a chest X-ray.

These tests are not only carried out to check for signs that what you have is angina, but also to rule out some of the non-cardiac causes of chest pain that we looked at earlier in this chapter.

More detailed investigation will then be carried out. These will be coordinated by a heart specialist (cardiologist) in your local hospital and may well take place in a dedicated acute chest pain clinic.

This next set of tests will be used to confirm the diagnosis and then to establish which of your coronary arteries are the narrowed troublemakers. A plan can then be made about the best treatment for your symptoms.

The specific tests you might be put through, which we have looked at in more detail in Chapter 2, are:

- myocardial perfusion scan
- MRI/CT scan
- angiogram
- echocardiogram
- exercise ECG.

Drugs used to treat angina

Once the diagnosis has been made, treatment can be started. The aim of this will be to cut down on the number and severity of future angina attacks (and to stop them altogether if possible), to act as prevention of heart attacks and strokes, and to generally improve quality of life.

The types of treatment used will vary depending on how severe the symptoms are. They will include: medication, stenting of coronary arteries, and full-on heart surgery.

The table below gives an idea of the most common types of medicine someone with angina might be prescribed, along with the reason each drug is chosen.

Drug	Reason prescribed
Beta blockers (e.g. bisoprolol)	These drugs make the heart beat slower and less forcefully, which reduces the demand of heart muscle for blood and oxygen.
Calcium channel blockers (e.g. verapamil)	These relax the walls of blood vessels supplying the heart muscle and so improve blood flow to them.
Short-acting nitrates (e.g. GTN)	In an acute angina attack this drug, which is used as a spray or tablet under the tongue, also dilates blood vessels supplying the heart, increasing blood flow.
Long-acting nitrates (e.g. isosorbide mononitrate)	These drugs have the same effect as GTN but are designed to be more long-lasting.
Nicorandil	This drug activates potassium channel receptors in coronary blood vessel walls, which again causes them to dilate and so improves blood flow to heart muscle.
Ivabradine	This drug works a bit like beta blockers by slowing down the heart rate.

Ranolazine	This new medication works on heart muscles themselves. It seems to cause them to relax, which improves blood flow.

Preventative medicines used in angina

Alongside the drugs that are prescribed specifically to treat angina attacks, other drugs will also be prescribed. These are designed to help prevent the changes in blood vessels that cause angina (the atherosclerosis mentioned above) from getting worse and putting the person at risk of having a heart attack or stroke.

These pills include drugs to thin the blood and reduce cholesterol levels, the main examples of which are aspirin and statins respectively.

Aspirin

This drug has been shown to reduce the stickiness of platelets in the blood which, when they clump together, form blood clots. Platelet clumping is more likely to happen when the internal walls of blood vessels have ragged edges, as they do when atherosclerosis has developed. Blood clots forming on already furred-up arteries narrow them even further, making a total blockage possible. If a coronary artery becomes totally blocked a heart attack will happen pretty soon after. People often refer to this mechanism of preventing blood clots as thinning the blood.

Statins

This group of drugs, which includes atorvastatin and simvastatin, works by blocking the effect of an enzyme in the liver which produces cholesterol. Alongside reducing cardiac risk by lowering the levels of cholesterol in the blood, statins also have direct effects on already established areas of atherosclerosis, first by reducing the cholesterol inside them and second by making them more stable.

Angioplasty and stenting

If the drugs don't work and the symptoms of angina continue unremittingly or the narrowing of arteries to the heart is found to be so severe that all the pills in the world are unlikely to prevent a heart attack, then these procedures can help restore blood flow to the heart by stretching out critically narrowed coronary arteries.

Angioplasty, which is carried out under local anaesthetic, involves inserting a small catheter into the groin, wrist, or arm and carefully guiding it through blood vessels all the way to the heart under X-ray guidance. Once it reaches the narrowed artery a balloon at the tip of the catheter is inflated. This opens up the artery by squashing fatty deposits back against its walls.

Very often a stent is placed over the balloon before the catheter is inserted. This expands when the balloon is inflated and will remain in place to act like internal scaffolding when the balloon is deflated and removed.

Surgery

If two or more coronary arteries are narrowed or either of the most vital arteries (left anterior descending and left coronary) are too severely narrowed for stenting, surgery may need to be performed. The operation carried out is called coronary artery bypass grafting or CABG for short. Thanks to its acronym, doctors often refer to this procedure as a cabbage (CABbaGe).

As its name suggests it involves grafting other blood vessels onto the coronary arteries to bypass the narrowed regions and restore blood flow. The most commonly used vessels are the internal thoracic arteries, which are found inside the chest wall behind the rib cage. Another, now less commonly used, vessel is the saphenous vein, which is stripped from the inside of the patient's leg.

This is, perhaps not surprisingly, a major operation, which can take anywhere between three and six hours to perform and is carried out under general anaesthetic.

Researchers who have compared the long-term effects of stents and CABG surgery on patients with angina have found that while one month after their procedures patients with stents report being in better health than those who have been operated on, this situation has reversed at six months, with CABG patients experiencing less angina and better quality of life.

Heart attack

Finally we come to what is probably the most infamous and widely feared of all causes of chest pain: the heart attack, or in medical parlance a myocardial infarction.

This occurs when there's a total blockage of one of the coronary arteries, starving an area of heart muscle of oxygen. If left long enough without treatment this area of muscle will die, which at best will be life-limiting and at worst, fatal. A heart attack is therefore a medical emergency.

A few facts and figures

According to the British Heart Foundation, around 200,000 people in the UK will have a heart attack every year (that's one every three minutes!). In the USA the annual figure is 1.5 million people.

Thankfully, survival rates are on the up, so while in the 1960s seven out of ten heart attacks in the UK proved fatal, the odds are much better with seven out of ten people now surviving. However, this obviously means that 30 per cent of people don't, so it's still vital for all of us to follow the advice in this book and look after our hearts, and just as vital for

 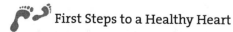

anyone experiencing symptoms of a heart attack to call for an ambulance immediately.

What are the symptoms?

Symptoms will include some or all of the following:

- chest pain which is invariably behind the breastbone in the centre of the chest and is commonly described as heavy, crushing, tight, burning, and sometimes sharp. This pain is generally, although not always, intense and lasts between thirty minutes and one hour
- other associated pains which can occur in the neck, jaw, left shoulder, and down the left arm
- shortness of breath
- sweating and clamminess
- nausea and sometimes vomiting
- giddiness or light-headedness.

How is it diagnosed?

The diagnosis is usually made in hospital, but as GPs we still see people with chest pain in our clinics who, not wanting to bother the ambulance service, have booked an appointment with us. So the initial diagnosis is sometimes made in the GP surgery, with the doctor calling for the ambulance once the diagnosis is made (and praying that it arrives quickly).

Once the doctor, nurse, or paramedic has ascertained symptoms and made a physical examination, there are a few crucial tests which help confirm what's going on. These are an electrocardiogram (ECG) and blood tests.

The ECG (explained in Chapter 3) will be used to look for specific changes which signify that the heart is struggling for oxygen. The most significant of these is a rise in the ST segment of an ECG known as ST elevation. An ST elevation myocardial infarction (STEMI) is more serious than other types and action needs to be taken as an emergency. If there's no ST elevation, then the heart attack will be categorized as the less serious non-ST elevation myocardial infarction (NSTEMI).

Alongside an ECG a number of blood tests will be performed. One of the most helpful is a test looking for raised levels of a protein called troponin.

Troponin is involved in enabling heart muscle to contract and is normally only found in very low levels in the bloodstream. If heart muscle is damaged, as it is during a heart attack, then more troponin is released into the blood. And the more severe the heart attack, the higher the level rises.

The troponin level will rise between three and twelve hours after a heart attack and stay elevated for up to two weeks. However, in many people the level won't rise within the first six hours, so troponin will be tested on arrival in hospital and then ten to twelve hours later in order not to miss a possible rise.

Immediate treatment

The key to treatment of a heart attack is to receive it as quickly as possible in order to reduce the amount of damage that is done, with the exact type of treatment given depending on whether you are having a STEMI or NSTEMI, the time that's passed since the chest pain came on, and your general state of health. The aim of this treatment will be to try and get blood flowing to the heart muscle again. This might involve one of two methods: angioplasty and stenting (which we've looked at earlier in the chapter) or thrombolysis.

With thrombolysis the idea is to break up the clot blocking the coronary artery. This is done using injections of drugs such as streptokinase and alteplase. These have been designed to break down a protein called fibrin, which holds blood clots together.

Long-term treatment

The aims of treatment after a heart attack are to:

- help you recover and get back to living as normal a life as possible
- help prevent you from having another one.

And we'll end this chapter looking at how healthcare professionals can help you achieve these goals.

Recovery

A few weeks after discharge from hospital you will be invited to attend a course of cardiac rehabilitation. This course will include a mixture of information and exercise to help you get your head around what's gone on and to get you back on your feet again.

The team running the course may include doctors, specialist nurses, physiotherapists, dietitians, psychologists, and occupational therapists. They will be able to use their expertise to help you:

- understand your condition and the medicines used to treat it
- get over the psychological impact of a severe health scare
- make changes to your lifestyle that will help keep you healthy and reduce the risk of recurrences
- develop a sensible exercise regime.

These courses aren't just for people who've had a heart attack; they have been shown to help anyone with a serious heart condition.

Prevention

Alongside the advice that you'll pick up in the cardiac rehabilitation course about prevention of further heart attacks, your specialist will discharge you with a number of medicines that should help with this. Many of these are the same as those used to treat angina which we came across earlier in the chapter, like aspirin, beta blockers, statins, and calcium channel blockers. But, in addition, you are likely to be given a stronger blood thinner to go alongside your aspirin for a year afterwards.

This group of drugs includes the medicines clopidogrel and ticagrelor. They stop platelets from clumping together and prevent further blood clots forming in both the coronary arteries and the circulation in general, so cut down the risk of a further heart attack or a stroke.

5
Trouble with valves

As we saw in Chapter 1, there are four valves in the heart, called the aortic, mitral, pulmonary, and tricuspid valves. Each of these valves has flaps which open and close with each heartbeat to ensure that blood passes through the heart and around the body in one direction. If these valves become diseased or damaged then blood won't flow as it should do and symptoms can develop.

There are two main ways in which problems with valves can affect blood flow:

- Regurgitation – the valve does not close properly and the blood will flow backwards.
- Stenosis – the valve does not open properly and blood flow is restricted.

The outcome in both cases is that the heart starts to pump inefficiently. This puts extra strain on the heart and that's when symptoms develop.

What causes valve disease?

Age

Heart valve disease can occur as part of the ageing process. As we get older, valves can become thickened, causing stenosis, or stretched, causing them to be floppier.

These changes can be made more likely if you have had certain infections (endocarditis and rheumatic fever), a heart attack, a history of high blood pressure, high cholesterol, and diabetes.

Birth abnormalities

Some babies are born with valve problems. Many of these are now picked up in the womb during antenatal scans and some can actually be treated before birth.

Cardiomyopathy

Both dilated and hypertrophic cardiomyopathies (see Chapter 7) can cause damage to heart valves.

What are the symptoms of valve disease?

The symptoms you experience will depend on which valves are affected and how badly. They can include all or some of the following:

- shortness of breath at rest and when you're exerting yourself
- shortness of breath lying flat. This symptom, called orthopnoea, is often assessed by doctors by asking how many pillows you need to sleep on
- waking in the night short of breath
- swollen feet and ankles
- palpitations
- chest pains

- tiredness
- dizziness and fainting.

How is valve disease diagnosed?

The diagnostic process will begin with a consultation in your GP surgery and then if needed involve tests in the surgery followed by more detailed investigations in hospital.

Clinical evaluation

First of all, your doctor or nurse will want to ask about your symptoms: how long you've been having them, when you get them, how often you get them, and anything that makes them better or worse.

They will then examine you. They will look to see whether you have swollen feet or ankles, check your pulse rate and rhythm and your blood pressure.

Next they will listen to your heart. The blood flow through diseased valves will usually generate a sound called a murmur, which doctors can pick up using a stethoscope (you won't hear it yourself).

If your symptoms and their clinical examination findings suggest a problem with your valves, they will arrange further tests.

Simple tests

They are likely to advise you to have some blood tests to check for the risk factors of heart disease. These will include your blood sugar and cholesterol levels, kidney and liver function, and a full blood count.

They may also request a test for a protein called B-type natriuretic peptide (BNP). If the valves are malfunctioning to the extent that you are developing what's called heart failure (where the heart is unable to pump blood around the body properly), the level of this protein will be high.

Other basic tests they will want to carry out will include an ECG and a chest X-ray (see Chapter 3).

Echocardiogram

They will no doubt also refer you to a hospital radiology (X-ray) department for an echocardiogram. This is a special type of ultrasound, much like expectant mothers have during pregnancy, except that instead of checking on a developing baby inside the womb the scan is used to look at how well the heart is pumping and at the structure and function of the valves.

In some cases doctors will want to carry out a more detailed transoesophageal echocardiogram, where, under sedation, a probe is passed down your oesophagus (gullet) to get a closer view of the nearby heart. Other people may be requested to have a cardiac MRI scan (for more details on these tests see Chapter 3).

Treatment

Many people with mild heart valve disease don't need treatment. They will have regular check-ups, and doctors may also be able to help reduce the impact of symptoms with a variety of medications.

If you are in this situation, then your doctor will no doubt also advise you to try and adopt lifestyle changes (detailed in Chapter 9) which aim to keep your heart as healthy as possible. These include stopping smoking, drinking safe levels of alcohol, taking regular exercise, and adopting a healthy, balanced diet.

For those with more severe symptoms, the main treatment will be surgical, involving an operation.

 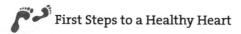

Medical treatments

A variety of medications can be prescribed that will be aimed at keeping symptoms at bay, helping the heart to work more efficiently in order to prevent complications such as blood clots forming on diseased valves. The table below shows some examples of the medications that you might be prescribed.

Type of drug	Example	Action
Diuretics (water tablets)	Furosemide	Reduce the amount of fluid in the tissues and the blood vessels. This eases workload on the heart and can help with symptoms like breathlessness.
Angiotensin converting enzyme (ACE) inhibitors	Ramipril	Cause blood vessels to dilate, which lowers blood pressure and allows the heart to pump more effectively.
Beta blockers	Bisoprolol	Slow the heart rate, which reduces the heart's workload. They also lower blood pressure and can help treat palpitations.
Anticoagulants (blood thinners)	Warfarin	Reduce the risk of blood clots forming on damaged valves, which could break off and cause strokes.

Surgical treatments

If surgery to the valves is needed this can take one of two main forms:

* repair
* replacement.

Trouble with valves **53**

The choice of which procedure is performed will depend on the degree of damage to your valve.

Repair
This is most often used for the treatment of regurgitation of the mitral valve but can also be used for when valves have become too tight (stenosed).

Where the mitral valve is concerned the operation will be carried out either through a cut in the breastbone or a smaller one through the ribs. Once inside, the surgeon will partially sew the flaps of the valve together to stop blood flowing the wrong way.

For a stenosed valve, particularly the aortic valve, repair may be possible using a balloon. The process is the same as in cardiac catheterization and once inside the tightened aortic valve the balloon is dilated in order to stretch it.

Replacement
If the valve can't be repaired, then it may be possible to replace it.

There are two kinds of replacement valve used in this type of surgery:

1. Artificial valves. These are made of carbon and metal and are long-lasting, but people with these will need to have lifelong anticoagulant medication to stop blood clots forming.

2. Tissue valves. These are made from pig or cow tissue that's been specially treated to be safe for humans. You don't need to take lifelong blood thinners if you have one of these, but the downside is that they wear out more quickly than artificial valves and have to be changed every ten to twenty years.

 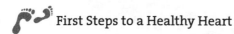

The operation itself is carried out under general anaesthetic (you are asleep) and it involves the surgeon cutting through your breastbone to expose your heart. They then stop your heart beating so they can work on it while it's still, and all your vital circulatory functions are then taken over by what's called a bypass machine. Once the valve is replaced, you come off bypass and are stitched back together again.

The operation usually takes a few hours and you will be closely monitored in hospital for about a week afterwards. Recovery will take up to three months.

Sometimes aortic valves can be replaced without the need for a large cut through your breastbone in a procedure called a transcatheter aortic valve implant (TAVI). As its name implies, this procedure again involves the use of a catheter, which is passed up to your heart through an artery in either your wrist or under your collarbone. Once inside the damaged valve a balloon is inflated to open the damaged valve up and a new one is then placed inside it. The balloon is then deflated, leaving the new valve in place inside the old one.

Complications of heart valve disease

While many people with heart valve disease don't run into any trouble, there are a few potential complications that can arise, some of which we have already looked at:

- heart failure
- abnormal rhythms
- formation of blood clots causing strokes.

A final complication is the possibility of a specific type of infection called endocarditis.

What is endocarditis?

Endocarditis is an infection that is usually caused by bacteria in your bloodstream. If you have damaged or diseased valves, these bacteria can stick to them and start to multiply. This type of infection is difficult to fight off and is potentially life threatening.

What are the symptoms?

The symptoms can be quite vague, therefore difficult to pick up. In fact, it can just feel like a dose of the flu with fever, achiness, weight loss, chills, and chest pain. But if you have these symptoms and know you have a damaged or repaired heart valve, you need to seek urgent medical advice.

How is it treated?

You will need to be admitted to hospital for high-dose intravenous antibiotics.

Can it be prevented?

One of the most common routes through which bacteria can enter the bloodstream is during dental surgery, so for many years people at risk of endocarditis due to valve disease were given antibiotics before their treatment. This is not now considered necessary for most people, but doctors may prescribe antibiotics prior to treatment if you have had endocarditis before.

If you take a cholesterol-lowering drug you can eat what you like.

Cholesterol in our bodies comes from two main sources: some is made in the liver and the rest comes from some of the food we eat. Drugs like statins that are taken to lower cholesterol levels work on the cholesterol made in the liver. So if you continue to eat foods that are high in cholesterol your levels will not go down and may even go up.

6
Electrical problems (arrhythmias)

In Chapter 1 we saw how the heart has an electrical system which kick-starts its pumping action in much the same way as a car engine has an electrical ignition to get it started. Both can malfunction, and while a breakdown service might have your car back on the road in a jiffy, it's a bit trickier when it comes to your heart.

The most catastrophic electrical malfunction is a cardiac arrest, when the heart stops beating altogether. This, it will hopefully not surprise you, is pretty incompatible with life and if the heart is not restarted promptly using a defibrillator to deliver a high-energy shock, it can be fatal.

But there are many other types of electrical problem that while not leading to imminent death can nevertheless cause some significantly disabling symptoms if left untreated. In this chapter we will look at some of the most common to see how they might affect us and how, if possible, they can be fixed.

Atrial fibrillation

This is by far the most common type of heart arrhythmia. It is believed to affect around 1 per cent of the total population and while rare in younger people it becomes more common as we get older, affecting around 5 per cent of those over sixty-five and 10 per cent of the over eighties.

What is it?

Atrial fibrillation occurs because cells in the walls of the atria of the heart start to produce uncoordinated electrical signals alongside the normal signals produced by the sinoatrial node (see Chapter 1). These abnormal signals make the walls of the atria twitch or, to use more technical parlance, fibrillate, hence the condition's name.

Because of this abnormal electrical activity the heart beats irregularly and usually more rapidly than it should. So when you feel someone's pulse, instead of being nicely spaced beats like the pattern below, where B indicates a heartbeat:

B   B   B   B   B   B   B   B

you get what's called an irregularly irregular pulse, where there's absolutely no set pattern at all and there are more beats every minute:

BBB   B   B B   BB   B   B   BB B B

What causes it?

There are a number of different conditions that can cause the atria to fibrillate like this, which were all drummed into us as medical students. Examples of these include:

• high blood pressure

- heart attacks
- heart valve problems
- previous heart surgery
- an overactive thyroid gland
- stimulant chemicals such as caffeine and alcohol
- pneumonia
- obstructive sleep apnoea
- obesity.

Depending on the cause, atrial fibrillation can either be occasional (paroxysmal), when it will come and go, or persistent, hanging around permanently to become your new "normal" heartbeat.

What are the symptoms?
While some people don't have any symptoms, most will notice one or more of the following, which will often cause them to book a trip to see their doctor:
- palpitations (the sensation of a racing, irregular heartbeat)
- shortness of breath (at rest but most often on exertion)
- chest pains
- episodes of dizziness, light-headedness, or feeling faint
- tiredness.

How is it diagnosed?
Your GP, or if it's severe enough a doctor in a hospital, will often be able to pick it up by simply taking your pulse, where the characteristic irregularly irregular pattern described above will be enough to point towards atrial fibrillation as the cause of your symptoms. They will also listen to the sound of your heart and lungs and check your blood pressure to get a fuller picture of what's going on.

But the clincher will be the ECG (see Chapter 3), as atrial fibrillation produces a classic pattern which emerges on the heart tracing.

Doctors will also check bloods, looking for an underlying cause such as a heart attack or an overactive thyroid gland, and if you're out of breath with it they might also send you for a chest X-ray, looking for any signs of fluid build-up on your lungs.

Is it dangerous?

If left untreated atrial fibrillation can potentially put you at high risk of having a stroke or developing heart failure.

The stroke risk is raised by around five or six times (compared to someone without fibrillation) because the fibrillating atria don't pump blood efficiently, so it tends to pool in their chambers leading to the possibility of clots developing within them. If these form and are then pumped around the body they will become lodged when they reach blood vessels that are too small for them. This consequently creates a dam, blocking the flow of blood behind it and starving the tissues downstream of oxygen. When this happens in the brain it will cause a stroke.

The heart itself can become less effective at pumping because of long-term atrial fibrillation. This means that blood doesn't circulate as well as it should, resulting in a condition called heart failure. Here fluid can build up in the lungs, causing breathlessness, and in the ankles and legs, causing swelling.

How is it treated?

There are three main aspects to the treatment of atrial fibrillation:

1. Improving the rhythm.
2. Controlling the heart rate.
3. Stroke prevention.

Improving the rhythm

This can be attempted using the following methods:

- Drug treatment. Medicines including sotalol, flecainide, and amiodarone can be used, with the choice depending on any other pills you take and your other pre-existing medical conditions.
- Cardioversion. This is a procedure carried out in hospital under general anaesthetic, which involves giving you a controlled electric shock to try and restore a normal rhythm.
- Catheter ablation. Here a catheter is inserted into one of your blood vessels in either your wrist or groin from where it is passed under X-ray guidance towards your heart. Once in place radiofrequency energy is used to destroy the area of heart tissue causing the arrhythmia.
- Pacemaker. This is a battery-operated device that's implanted in your chest just under your collarbone. It produces electrical signals which aim to help the heart beat more regularly.

Controlling the heart rate

The mainstay of treatment for regulating the heart rate is medication, the most well known of which is probably the drug digoxin which was originally derived from the foxglove plant.

Newer drugs that are now more commonly used are beta blockers like bisoprolol, and calcium channel blockers including verapamil.

Stroke prevention

The key factor where preventing strokes is concerned is to stop the blood from clotting inside the fibrillating chambers of the heart. The medicines used to do this are called anticoagulants, although they are most commonly known as drugs to "thin the blood". And although they don't actually do that it is an easy way of understanding why these pills are prescribed.

The most well-known "blood-thinning" drug is probably warfarin. It's the most commonly used around the world and has the dubious heritage of being first used as rat poison when designed in the USA in 1948.

The process of blood clotting involves a complicated set of chemical reactions, and warfarin blocks one of these reactions so that it takes much longer for the blood to clot. It's perhaps not surprising that one of the main side effects of warfarin is bleeding, and people taking it will often bruise very easily and bleed for much longer if they cut or graze themselves.

Another problem with warfarin is that it can interact with lots of other medicines and be affected by diet and alcohol intake. And despite the fact that its level in the blood is always measured with regular blood tests, it can still be difficult to control its level in some people, making uncontrolled bleeding (from the bowel, from cuts, and perhaps nosebleeds) a real risk.

In 2011 a new group of blood-thinning drugs called NOACs (novel oral anticoagulants) was introduced. These pills, of which apixaban and rivaroxaban are examples, have a far more predictable effect on clotting and so carry much less risk of dangerous bleeding than warfarin. And they come with the added bonus that people taking them do not have to be subjected to regular blood tests to monitor their effects.

Supraventricular tachycardia (SVT)

In this arrhythmia the heart rhythm is normal but the rate is abnormally fast. So where an average resting pulse is between 60 and 100 beats per minute, in SVT the rate is over 100 beats per minute and very often will go as high as 250 beats per minute.

What is it?
In SVT the heart rate is abnormally fast either because electrical impulses are produced too quickly (a condition called atrial tachycardia), or because there is a fault in the way that electrical impulses are conducted (atrioventricular nodal reentry tachycardia or Wolff-Parkinson-White syndrome).

Atrial tachycardia
This condition is the least common cause of SVT. It arises when an area of heart tissue in the atria starts to fire off its own electrical signals that are faster than those of the heart's natural pacemaker. It is often an intermittent problem but in some it can last for days.

Atrioventricular nodal reentry tachycardia (AVNRT)
AVNRT occurs because of a short circuit in the electrical conduction system near the atrioventricular node. Extra electrical impulses whizz around this extra circuit putting the pulse up.

Wolff-Parkinson-White syndrome (WPW)
In WPW there is an extra electrical pathway between the atria and ventricles, which can conduct extra impulses. These impulses are transmitted in addition to those from the heart's normal pacemaker and they are transmitted faster, again putting the pulse up.

What causes it?
SVT is more common in people in their twenties and thirties and in women more than men. It has a variety of possible triggers:
- medications including asthma inhalers
- stress

- alcohol and caffeine
- smoking.

What are the symptoms?
Symptoms will last only as long as the attack itself and will stop when it does. This is most often minutes or hours but may be longer. They will tend to start suddenly and can include:
- palpitations
- shortness of breath
- chest discomfort
- dizziness
- feeling faint.

How is it diagnosed?
It's usually diagnosed when an ECG is carried out during an attack and the doctor analyses the pattern of the heart tracing. If the attack has settled, your GP may refer you for an ambulatory ECG to try and capture the pattern of SVT during a longer reading.

Once diagnosed you are likely to be referred for electrophysiological tests on your heart to try and establish what the cause of your SVT is (e.g. WPW etc.).

Is it dangerous?
Most of the time SVT is completely harmless and some cases might not need treating at all because they settle on their own. But some WPW rhythms can be dangerous so treatment is invariably advised.

How is it treated?
If episodes are infrequent and your symptoms are mild, you may not need any long-term treatment. But your doctor will no

doubt advise you about avoiding possible triggers:

- smoking
- alcohol
- street drugs like ecstasy and cocaine
- over-the-counter cough medicines containing pseudoephedrine.

They may also teach you some simple self-help measures – like the Valsalva manoeuvre (see box below) and immersing your face in cold water – which can be tried during an attack in order to stop it.

Valsalva manœuvre

This is the fancy name for something we all do when we are either trying to "pop" our ears in an aeroplane or when we are, to use the vernacular, straining to have a poo.

It involves breathing out forcefully while closing your mouth and pinching your nose.

This increases the pressure in the sinuses, nose, throat, ears and eustachian tubes, chest, abdomen, and rectum, which in turn will not only make your ears "pop" and help you go to the toilet, but from an arrhythmia point of view will slow down your pulse and so bring an SVT under control.

If these simple measures don't do the trick then doctors may have to intervene to stop the abnormal heart rhythm. This is done either with intravenous medication or by giving the heart an electrical shock, procedures known as chemical and electrical cardioversion respectively.

Chemical cardioversion

There are two main drugs that can be injected to try and get the heart to revert back into a normal rhythm. The first choice is a drug called adenosine, which works by blocking the faulty electrical signals that are causing the arrhythmia.

A second drug that can be used is verapamil. This is not used for most people because although it's effective in correcting an arrhythmia it has a side effect of dropping blood pressure. Its main use is in people who also have asthma, who can't have adenosine as it can make their asthma worse.

Electrical cardioversion

If neither the Valsalva manoeuvre nor drugs mentioned above manage to get your heartbeat back to normal you may need electrical cardioversion. This is done using a defibrillator, which is the machine used to restart the heart during a cardiac arrest and which you'll no doubt have seen being used in TV medical dramas like *Casualty* and *ER*.

This simple, quick, and safe procedure is carried out while you're asleep under general anaesthetic and involves passing an electric current across your heart to shock it back into a normal rhythm.

Long-term treatment

Once your heart is behaving itself again, there are a couple of things that your doctor may suggest to prevent you having further episodes of SVT. The first of these is drug treatment using medicines such as beta blockers and verapamil to slow down the electrical impulses in your heart to stop them getting out of control again.

The second treatment is called catheter ablation. This is a very effective and more permanent solution to the problem, and it cures 95 per cent of people of their arrhythmia.

It is carried out in hospital under local anaesthetic. A cardiologist uses a catheter that's threaded through a vein in the groin and then on up to the heart, where the catheter can be used to identify the area of tissue responsible for the abnormal electrical impulses. This area is then destroyed using high frequency radio waves passed through the catheter tip.

Pacemakers

Pacemakers are little boxes (about the size of a matchbox) that can be implanted under your skin at the front of your chest. They are used to treat arrhythmias where the pulse is either too slow or too fast.

Wires from the pacemaker are attached to the heart. They sense if the pulse is abnormal and can then send out electrical impulses to correct it.

Implantable cardioverter defibrillators

These are boxes similar to pacemakers that detect if your heart has developed a dangerous arrhythmia that could potentially lead to cardiac arrest.

If they pick one up they deliver a shock to your heart that essentially reboots it and starts it beating in a safer rhythm.

7

When the muscle malfunctions

As we've seen in the previous chapters, the heart needs a good blood supply, a normally functioning electrical system, and efficient valves if it's going to work effectively as a pump. But there's one more vital component that also needs to be in tip-top condition if the heart is going to do its job properly, and that's the heart muscle itself.

The heart, after all, is basically a big lump of beating muscle and if this muscle fails then even with the best blood and electrical supplies and perfect valves, the pump will fail. So it's not hard to imagine how diseases of the heart muscle, called cardiomyopathies, can be a very real risk to health.

In this chapter we'll look at what these cardiomyopathies are, how they are diagnosed, the symptoms they cause, and what can be done about them.

There are three main cardiomyopathies:

1. Dilated cardiomyopathy.

2. Hypertrophic cardiomyopathy.

3. Arrhythmogenic right ventricular cardiomyopathy.

Often these conditions are inherited and so run in families. And it's thought that they affect around 1 in 500 people of any age in the UK.

Dilated cardiomyopathy

This is the most common type of cardiomyopathy, which affects 1 in 250 people. Here the walls of the left ventricle of the heart become stretched and the heart muscle becomes thinner, meaning that the heart isn't able to pump blood around the body as effectively.

What causes it?

This type of cardiomyopathy affects both adults and children and has a variety of causes:

- Around 30 per cent of people with this condition have inherited it because of a genetic mutation.
- An unhealthy lifestyle: people who have a diet that's low in vitamins and minerals, who drink too much alcohol, or use recreational (street) drugs are at risk.
- A viral infection, called myocarditis, which affects heart muscle can cause it.
- It can occur as a complication of pregnancy.
- It can be part of another condition, including systemic sclerosis, Wegener's granulomatosis, sarcoidosis, and muscular dystrophy.
- In many people the cause is unknown or, in medical parlance, idiopathic, which is Greek for "sorry, we haven't got a clue".

What are the symptoms?
Because it affects the way the heart pumps, many of the symptoms are the same as those for heart failure, like breathlessness, fatigue, and swollen ankles and legs.

It can also cause palpitations and chest pain.

How is it diagnosed?
Doctors will want to take a thorough history of symptoms and perform a clinical examination. Tests like an ECG and echocardiogram can help, and specialists may also carry out genetic tests to see if the condition is inherited.

How is it treated?
This condition can't be cured, so treatments are aimed at improving symptoms. These range from lifestyle changes to medications and surgery.

Lifestyle advice:
- Cut down on alcohol and caffeine.
- Watch your weight and eat a healthy, balanced diet.
- If you smoke – stop. If you don't smoke – don't start!
- Cut down the amount of salt in your diet.
- Moderate exercise may help, but this needs to be discussed with your cardiologist first.

Medication is aimed at reducing symptoms and preventing blood clots from forming in the circulation. So pills that are prescribed will often be aimed at reducing fluid overload (diuretics), keeping the heart rate regular (beta blockers and others), helping the heart pump more efficiently (beta blockers and ACE inhibitors), and thinning the blood (anticoagulants).

Surgery can range from insertion of devices like pacemakers

When the muscle malfunctions

to keep the heart beating regularly, all the way to the, rare, situation where someone needs a heart transplant.

Hypertrophic cardiomyopathy

This condition causes heart muscle to become thickened and stiffer. It's estimated that it affects around 1 in 500 people in the UK with most of them, thankfully, having very few symptoms and so not ever needing treatment.

What causes it?
It's a genetic condition that runs in families. A child of someone with it has a 50 per cent chance of inheriting it.

What are the symptoms?
Those who develop symptoms will again share them with people who have heart failure, so they may suffer with shortness of breath, palpitations, chest pain, dizziness, and fainting.

How is it diagnosed?
Once again the clinical history and examination will be the important starting point, followed by an ECG and echocardiogram. Your cardiologist may also arrange an MRI scan.

MRI (magnetic resonance imaging) scans are carried out inside tunnel-shaped scanners. Unlike a CT scan, these scans don't use radiation from X-rays to create images, but use magnetic and radio waves instead. These can build up detailed pictures of the body's tissues and internal organs, including heart muscle.

Genetic testing of the family may also be recommended.

How is it treated?
As with dilated cardiomyopathy, the treatment of hypertrophic

 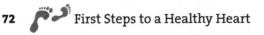

cardiomyopathy is aimed at alleviating symptoms and preventing complications. It relies on similar drugs and lifestyle advice and can also involve surgery to remove some of the thickened muscle in the heart.

Arrhythmogenic right ventricular cardiomyopathy (ARVC)

In this condition there's a problem with the proteins that hold heart muscle cells together. As a result these cells can die and are then replaced by fatty cells and scar tissue. It usually goes on to cause electrical conduction abnormalities and arrhythmias.

ARVC classically affects the right ventricle of the heart (see Chapter 1) but can also affect the left ventricle, when it is known by the more inclusive name of arrhythmic cardiomyopathy. It never affects the atria on either side.

What causes it?

Like the other cardiomyopathies this is an inherited order, but it's much less common, affecting around 1 in 10,000 people, most of whom are teenagers and young adults.

What are the symptoms?

The most common symptoms are again similar to the other myopathies: palpitations, shortness of breath, leg and ankle swelling, and fainting. But it can also cause some quite severe arrhythmias like ventricular fibrillation, which can be life threatening, and sudden cardiac death, which particularly affects athletes.

How is it diagnosed?

There are no prizes for guessing that a detailed clinical history and examination are a vital part of the assessment along with an

ECG and echocardiogram.

Other tests may include cardiac MRI scan, 24-hour ECG, and electrophysiology studies.

How is it treated?

Symptom management will involve the same drugs as the other cardiomyopathies and the lifestyle advice will also be the same. But particular treatments for this condition may include ablation of abnormal electrical pathways, pacemakers, or implantable cardioverter defibrillators (ICD).

ICDs identify abnormal heart rhythms that can be life threatening and deliver an electric shock to convert them back into normal rhythms.

Mythbuster

You can't really suffer with a broken heart.

It actually seems that you can.

In 2014 doctors from London published research in the well-respected journal *JAMA Internal Medicine* (published by the American Medical Association) which found that the number of people who died of a heart attack or stroke in the month after their partner died was double that of a group of people matched for both age and sex who weren't grieving.

There's also a condition called broken heart syndrome or takotsubo cardiomyopathy. Here there's a temporary weakness in the muscle of the heart as a direct response to a stressful event like the death of a spouse or relationship breakdown. Thankfully though, this condition is rarely life threatening and people often recover within a month.

8
High blood pressure (hypertension)

As family heirlooms go, the one that has been passed on to me is, I think you'll agree, pretty rubbish: high blood pressure.

It has probably already become clear from the anecdotes peppering other chapters in this book that when the good Lord was dishing out hearts most of my family were at the back of the queue where only the factory seconds were left to be installed. And much of the coronary disease that's afflicted us has had the ground laid for it by a strong family history of high blood pressure.

I, like my father before me, was only thirty when mine was diagnosed. Consequently I have now been swallowing blood pressure pills every day for the best part of the last twenty years.

But as a doctor I have seen far too many people who have not taken their hypertension seriously and suffered heart attacks or strokes (or even worse) as a result. So I'm quite the evangelist when it comes to telling people about the pitfalls of untreated high blood pressure and encouraging the lifestyle changes that can help us all reduce it. Because, let's face it, taking a bit more exercise, losing some weight, cutting down on cigarettes and booze, and even popping a pill or two every day are small sacrifices to make compared to the alternatives that unremitting hypertension has to offer.

In this chapter we'll look at what high blood pressure is, what can cause it, why it can be such bad news for us if not treated, and what those treatments are.

What is blood pressure?

As we saw in Chapter 1 the blood in the arteries in our circulatory system needs to be under a degree of pressure in order for it to reach all the way to our fingers and toes and all the vital organs in between. The pressure is highest each time the heart contracts, during what's termed systole, and drops slightly lower as the heart relaxes in between heart beats, a phase called diastole.

So you may well have noticed when you have had yours checked by a doctor or nurse (or seen it in a TV hospital drama) that they mention two numbers when taking blood pressure. These are the systolic and diastolic levels, with each pressure measured using slightly antiquated units of millimetres of mercury (mmHg).

For an adult, normal blood pressure has traditionally always been said to be 120 systolic and 80 diastolic, recorded as 120/80 and said 120 over 80. But as you'll see in the box opposite there is a range of readings within which blood pressure is believed to be normal.

Blood pressure category	Range*
Low blood pressure	Below 90/60
Normal blood pressure	90/60 to 120/80
Pre-high blood pressure	120/80 to 140/90
High blood pressure	Above 140/90

*These ranges are for an average, otherwise healthy, adult and will vary for people with other medical conditions like diabetes.[2]

What causes high blood pressure?

There are two main types of high blood pressure for which the causes are different. They are called:

- primary or essential hypertension
- secondary hypertension.

Primary hypertension

This is the most common type of high blood pressure, affecting 95 per cent of all the people who have hypertension. It tends to develop slowly over a number of years and has many underlying risk factors, although it's not triggered by any single specific disease or cause. These risk factors are detailed in the box below.

---

2   People with readings in the pre-high blood pressure category don't yet have hypertension but it's known that those whose pressures fall within this range are twice as likely to go on to develop high blood pressure in the future. The category has been created as a warning that lifestyle changes might be needed to stop it developing.

Risk factors for primary hypertension

Age: It is much more common from middle age onwards.

Sex: Men develop it earlier than women.

Family history: It tends to run in families.

Ethnic origin: It is more common in people with an African Caribbean background than in those from other ethnic groups.

Obesity: Being overweight or obese alters hormone levels and increases the work the heart has to do when pumping.

Lack of exercise: This makes cardiac function less efficient in general.

Smoking: Every cigarette smoked causes a temporary increase in blood pressure, and smoking is also partly responsible for causing narrowing of the arteries, which raises blood pressure in the longer term.

Alcohol: It's still uncertain exactly why drinking higher than recommended levels of alcohol causes hypertension, but it's believed to be due to a combination of its effects on both certain hormones and the sympathetic nervous system.

Too much salt: Salt encourages our bodies to retain fluid, which raises blood pressure.

Secondary hypertension

This is the much less common type of high blood pressure, which develops when it is triggered by another medical condition, disease, or medication. There are a number of well-known culprits that can cause it:

- kidney disorders such as polycystic kidney disease and chronic renal failure
- hormonal conditions like Cushing's syndrome and thyroid disease
- drug side effects, particularly the combined contraceptive pill and anti-inflammatory drugs such as ibuprofen
- pregnancy
- sleep apnoea (a condition where people stop breathing while they are asleep).

Given the range of conditions that can cause secondary hypertension it's not appropriate (and there's no space) to go into any detail about this type of high blood pressure in a "First Steps" book, so in the rest of this chapter we will focus solely on primary hypertension. But if you are ever diagnosed with high blood pressure your doctor will send you for tests to rule out these potential causes, as treatment of the underlying condition may often lead to the blood pressure settling back down into the normal range.

How do you know you have high blood pressure?

The simple answer is that very often you don't, because unlike most medical conditions there aren't any specific symptoms to alert you to the fact that you might be hypertensive. Most commonly the diagnosis will be made "out of the blue" during a blood pressure recording as part of a general check-up with a GP or practice nurse, or during a company medical. Optometrists can also pick up changes during a routine eye test that may point to the diagnosis.

How is the diagnosis made?

"One swallow does not a summer make" goes the old proverb. And it's the same with blood pressure: one high reading doesn't mean you have hypertension (because it can go up if you've had a stressful day, or if you're anxious about being at the doctors' surgery). But it's a sign that your nurse or doctor will want to take a more detailed look at you.

First, they'll want to repeat your blood pressure while you're with them, once or maybe twice more, to make sure the reading is genuine. And for some people, by the time they get to the last reading and they've had a relaxing chat with their nurse or doctor, things will be back to normal.

But for those whose readings are consistently high, the next step is likely to involve either being sent for 24-hour blood pressure monitoring or, if they have their own blood pressure machine, taking their own readings at home.

24-hour ambulatory blood pressure monitoring

This, as I recently experienced for myself, involves being fitted with a blood pressure cuff which is worn around the upper arm and is connected to a small, digital blood pressure monitor worn on a belt. This allows you to carry on with your normal daily routine while readings are taken day and night to give an idea of what your blood pressure is like overall in real life.

I personally didn't find it too irritating when the cuff repeatedly inflated, although it did wake me up a couple of times when I was asleep. But I caused it to go crazy when it tried to take a reading while I was cycling uphill on my way home from work.

Once the twenty-four hours is over, the machine is returned, the readings are downloaded, and your nurse or doctor will have an accurate picture of what your blood pressure is doing throughout the day and night. This is particularly helpful in differentiating between those with genuinely high blood pressure and those who have what's called white coat hypertension.

White coat hypertension (WCH)

This term dates back to the days when all doctors wore white coats, and describes a condition in a group of people whose blood pressure rises when they are in a clinical setting, like a hospital or GP surgery, but is actually completely normal in real life. Doctors now rarely wear white coats (even wearing a tie can be frowned upon as a potential infection risk) and most of the time blood pressure is taken by nurses, but the term is still useful, as misdiagnosing people who have WCH to be genuine hypertensives can lead to unnecessary treatment with drugs to lower what is actually normal blood pressure.

Further tests

Once you've been followed up after having these blood pressure recordings made and you've had the diagnosis of high blood pressure confirmed, you will undergo a few other simple tests to assess whether you have primary or secondary hypertension, whether there is any evidence of early damage to your heart and circulation because of your high blood pressure, and finally to assess the general state of your cardiovascular system.

This will involve having an ECG and blood tests to look at kidney and liver function, blood sugar levels, and your blood lipid profiles (cholesterol and triglycerides). Your doctor may also want to check the back of your eyes for signs of blood vessel damage there and to dipstick a sample of your urine to check for the presence of protein or red blood cells, which can both be a sign of a kidney problem.

Once all the results are back you will begin treatment. Although if your blood pressure is persistently sky high, treatment will begin straight away.

How is it treated?

Treatment of hypertension has two main strands to it: advice on lifestyle modifications to help you to help yourself control your blood pressure and to stop it getting worse, and prescribed medication.

Lifestyle modifications

If you are a teetotal, non-smoking exercise freak with less meat on you than a butcher's pencil, there may be little advice that can be offered. But if, like most of us, you are a bit out of shape, get your exercise operating the TV remote control or a games console, and wash down your daily ration of high fat, high carbohydrate food with a pint of beer or generous glass of white wine, then there will be plenty of changes to make.

And if you are a regular smoker, then you will certainly be in for a bit of an ear-bashing.

The main advice you will be given to help lower your blood pressure is likely to include:

- Trying to increase your exercise so that you do around thirty minutes five times per week. This can include taking brisk walks, cycling, swimming, dancing, and even mowing the lawn (unless of course you have a large garden and use a ride-on mower). It's even better if you can build an exercise regime into your normal day. This might mean walking or cycling to work, taking the stairs rather than the lift in the office, treating your dog to even longer walks, or simply taking a longer route to the shop to pick up your morning paper.

- Changes in diet. This advice will be aimed at encouraging you to eat more wholegrain foods, fish, poultry, nuts, fruit and vegetables, and low fat dairy products. On the flip side you will be encouraged to cut down on foods that are high in saturated fats, trans fats, salt, and sugar.
- Reducing alcohol consumption if it seems excessive.
- Cutting down on caffeinated drinks.
- Stopping smoking. Support will be offered to try and help you achieve this, as it is rarely that easy.
- Trying relaxation therapies.

Each of these modifications can help lower blood pressure and reduce the risk of heart disease and stroke. But they may not be enough on their own to bring your hypertension under control. In which case there are a number of medications that can be prescribed to try to help.

Blood pressure medications

The technical term for these pills is antihypertensives and there are a range of different types which can help. The choice of which to try will depend on a number of factors, including your age, ethnic background, other medical conditions you have (especially diabetes), and other medications you might be taking.

Sometimes your doctor will strike it lucky and the first tablet you try will not only suit you but also sort out your high blood pressure. More often, the dose may need adjusting, other pills may need to be tried instead (because the first either doesn't suit you because of its side effects, or doesn't work), or you may need to take one or two of these drugs in combination to treat your blood pressure successfully.

We are all different and very often need our treatments tailor-made rather than off the peg. So don't be alarmed if your doctor has to try a few medicines on you before getting your blood pressure back to normal. It doesn't necessarily mean you are a particularly difficult case, probably just unique.

The most commonly used medications fit neatly into categories beginning with the letters A, B, C and D, with those in groups A, C, and D being used as first-line treatments, although many people may still be on those in group B.

Angiotensin converting enzyme (ACE) inhibitors (e.g. ramipril and perindopril)

These drugs work by blocking the production of a chemical in the body called angiotensin II, which when it enters the bloodstream causes water retention and blood vessels to become narrower, both of which put blood pressure up.

Angiotensin receptor blockers (e.g. candesartan and irbesartan)

These medicines also work against the effects of angiotensin II, but rather than stopping its production they block its actions once it is released from the kidneys.

Beta blockers (e.g atenolol and bisoprolol)

This group of drugs works by blocking the actions of the hormones adrenaline and noradrenaline which put up your pulse and make your heart beat more forcefully. They also block angiotensin II release from your kidneys.

Calcium channel blockers (e.g. amlodipine and diltiazem)

The walls of blood vessels contain smooth muscle cells. Calcium causes these muscles to contract and when they do the vessels narrow, putting up the pressure inside them. This group

 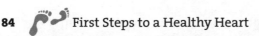

of drugs blocks the calcium, the muscle relaxes and pressure drops.

Diuretics (e.g. bendroflumethiazide and indapamide)

Diuretics work on your kidneys causing them to flush out more salt and water from your system. This lowers the blood pressure and has led to them having the nickname "water tablets", as they make you urinate more.

Long-term outlook

Once treatment is started you will be seen regularly by your practice nurse or GP to keep an eye on how it is going and to monitor any side effects you're experiencing. They will continue to follow you up and adjust your treatment until things are stable, when they will see you less frequently.

Once started, you are likely to be on this medication for the rest of your life. But popping a pill or two every day to reduce your hypertension is definitely worth it. A study in 2016 found that for every 10 mmHg drop in blood pressure on treatment, there is a 20 per cent drop in risk of a major cardiac event, such as a heart attack, and a 13 per cent drop in the risk of an early death.

So the take-home message is: keep taking the tablets!

You know you have high blood pressure because you get headaches and nosebleeds.

This is not the case for most people, who are blissfully unaware that their blood pressure is up, as it doesn't tend to cause symptoms. In very rare cases when the blood pressure is persistently, severely high (180/110 or even higher), then this may well produce a headache but otherwise recurrent headaches and nosebleeds are more likely to be a symptom of something else, so you should get them checked out by your family doctor.

9
Looking after your heart

Given that this book is called *First Steps to a Healthy Heart* it would be a bit strange, after all the chapters describing the problems you can have with your heart, if there wasn't advice on how to avoid all this trouble in the first place.

So this chapter is all about the good news that you can actually do things to help you to have a healthy heart. And you can do things to stop existing conditions getting worse as well.

Even if you are unfortunate enough to have one of the inherited heart conditions that you can't prevent, there's evidence that by following the advice in this chapter, you have a good chance of minimizing the effect these conditions can have on your life too.

So hopefully this chapter will have something for everyone, especially as it's never too late to benefit from the lifestyle changes that will be suggested.

They're not a quick fix, and won't act like a magic wand to undo overnight all the harm you may have done to your body through bad diet and lack of exercise. They are long-term changes rather than short-term fads and need to be worked at and to become part of your lifestyle for good.

But given the conditions you're hoping to avoid or make better, it's surely got to be worth a shot.

Risk factors

Figures from the World Health Organization (WHO) show that heart disease is the leading cause of death on the planet, with almost 18 million people dying every year. This equates to a phenomenal 31 per cent of all deaths around the globe every twelve months.

The major risk factors it lists for this are:

- an unhealthy diet
- lack of physical exercise
- smoking.

Alongside these, your risk of developing heart disease will increase if you also have diabetes and/or high blood pressure. So in addition to advice on modifying these lifestyle factors, the WHO also suggests regular check-ups with a doctor or nurse to monitor the risk factors that only health professionals can check: blood pressure, blood sugar, and cholesterol levels.

In this chapter we'll look at each of these risk factors and how to manage them.

What is a healthy diet?

In 2016 the UK government launched its "Eatwell Guide" which, based on research evidence and recommendations from a number of healthcare organizations, including the WHO, pretty much answered this question.

Fruit and vegetables

These are a rich source of vitamins and minerals (essential for maintaining the healthy structure and function of the body) and fibre (which helps regulate good digestion).

It's advised that over one-third of our diet should come from fruit and vegetables made up of at least five 80-gram portions: the so-called "five-a-day".

So, all meals should include fruit and vegetables, and it's a great idea to have fruit and raw vegetables, like carrots, as snacks between meals.

Although fruit juices and smoothies are advertised as being part of your "five-a-day", they are also full of sugar and can cause tooth decay, so should be limited to only one 150-millilitre drink per day.

Carbohydrates

This food group includes potatoes, rice, pasta, bread, and breakfast cereals.

Carbohydrates are broken down in our bodies during the digestion process to make smaller sugars, which we use for energy.

The Eatwell Guide suggests that while these should form the basis of each main meal we have, we should try to have wholegrain pasta, brown rice, and skin-on potatoes, as these contain more fibre and are richer in nutrients than white rice and pasta.

Proteins

Foods that are rich in protein include meat, fish, eggs, pulses (like lentils), and beans.

We need proteins for building and repairing our body's tissues and making hormones and antibodies, so it's suggested that we eat a source of protein every day and have some fish at least twice a week.

White meats like chicken are healthier and the advice is that we should consume no more than 70 grams of red or processed meats (like sausages and bacon) per day.

Try to buy lean cuts of meat, or cut off the fat, and grill or steam meat and fish rather than fry it.

High-fat foods

Foods that are high in fat and sugar include cakes, biscuits, sweets, chocolate bars, puddings, and ice cream.

There's no reason not to have these as a treat, but a treat is only a treat if it's had occasionally and not as an everyday part of the diet. So, in general, these foods should be consumed infrequently and in small quantities.

Dairy products

It's good to have some dairy products in the diet because milk and foods like cheese and yoghurt are good sources of protein and calcium.

But try to stick to low fat cheeses and yoghurts, and drink either skimmed or semi-skimmed milk.

Oils and spreads

Although we need some fat in the diet, unsaturated fats in cooking oils and spreads (e.g. margarine) are a healthier option.

Salt

Salt has been shown to raise blood pressure, so eating lots of salty foods and liberally sprinkling table salt over everything on our plates is not a good idea.

The recommended salt intake for an adult is 6 grams, which is about the amount you'd get on a teaspoon.

And it's important to remember that plenty of foods like ham, anchovies, bacon, cheese, pickles, olives, and stock cubes already contain high levels, so they don't need any extra salt with them at all.

Fluids

It's important to stay well hydrated and it's reckoned that adults should drink the equivalent of around six to eight glasses (or 1.2 litres) of water per day. This can include cups of tea and coffee but not high-calorie fizzy drinks.

Alcohol

Drinking too much alcohol can affect the heart because of weight gain, a rise in blood pressure, and an increased risk of arrhythmias.

The recommended intake in the UK for both men and women is 14 units per week. This should be spread over seven days with at least a couple of days per week being alcohol free.

Getting physical

Although Australian singer Olivia Newton-John's 1981 hit "Let's Get Physical" wasn't strictly about the kind of physical activity the WHO is advising for a healthy heart, it's not a bad mantra to have as a reminder that we all need to get some exercise.

But how does exercise help? What types of exercise are advisable? And how often should we be doing them?

The benefits of exercise

Exercise can help the heart both directly and indirectly in many ways:

- burns calories and helps with weight loss
- lowers blood pressure
- regulates blood sugar and helps reduce the risk of diabetes
- helps control cholesterol levels
- reduces stress hormones.

Which exercises?

For many people exercise means heading to the gym, pool, tennis court, or running track. And if you're able to, these obvious types of exercise, from jogging and swimming to team sports, are an ideal way to get your exercise.

But even if Lycra's not for you, there are plenty of other ways to get some exercise. In fact, research has shown that you can achieve the same effective levels of exercise in your DIY overalls, mowing the lawn, or while whizzing a vacuum cleaner around the home.

In the PURE study, published in the medical journal *The Lancet* in 2017, researchers looked at the benefits of a variety of both recreational (e.g. jogging, swimming, and tennis) and non-recreational activities for the cardiovascular health of over 130,000 people.

They found that all types of exercise, from playing squash to doing housework, gardening, a physical occupation, and walking or cycling to work, were all good for the heart and that the more exercise you do, the more the benefit. In fact, those who adhered to the current recommended amount of daily exercise had a 22 per cent lower chance of death or significant cardiovascular disease event (e.g. heart attack) than those who led a sedentary life.

How much exercise?

The cardiac benefits of physical activity that were found in the PURE study came when people undertook 150 minutes of moderate exercise per week. That's just thirty minutes per day on five days of each week. And the thirty minutes don't even all have to be together.

So what's stopping you when there are so many ways to keep active?

Smoking

Smokers are at least twice as likely to have a heart attack as non-smokers. And recent research has shown that smoking only one cigarette per day greatly increases your risk of developing heart disease to 48 per cent higher than people who have never smoked (*British Medical Journal*, 2018).

So if you smoke, the best thing you can do for your heart is to stop. And if you don't smoke, then whatever you do, don't start.

How does smoking affect your heart?

Most of us are aware of the ways smoking affects the lungs, triggering cancer and leaving people gasping for breath and dependent on inhalers and oxygen thanks to chronic bronchitis and emphysema. But smoking doesn't stop there; it has other pathological mischief to make, not least in our circulatory system:

- It damages the lining of blood vessels, leading to the build-up of atheroma.
- It makes the blood more likely to form clots inside your bloodstream.
- The carbon monoxide you breathe in reduces oxygen supply to the heart and makes it work harder.

- It makes blood vessel walls less elastic and stretchy, putting up blood pressure.
- Nicotine raises adrenaline levels, which also puts up blood pressure as well as making the heart beat unnecessarily faster.

Benefits of quitting
Stopping smoking has many positive effects, which can be either short or long term:
- Within twenty minutes pulse and blood pressure drop.
- Within twelve hours the level of carbon monoxide is back to normal.
- Between two and twelve weeks the circulation improves.
- After twelve months the risk of developing heart disease is 50 per cent lower than a smoker's.
- After fifteen years the risk of developing heart disease is back to that of a non-smoker.
- Stopping smoking after a heart attack reduces your chances of having another one by 50 per cent.

(Source: WHO website)

How do you quit?
Thankfully, given the many benefits of quitting, there's lots of help out there to support you through the process. And in the UK this can be accessed on the NHS through your GP or practice nurse.

For more detailed advice, please see Lion Hudson's book *First Steps out of Smoking*, but the list below gives you a flavour of what's on offer:
- Nicotine replacement therapies: From gum to inhalators, patches and lozenges, these can help reduce the cravings for nicotine in cigarettes once you've stopped. The strength of

 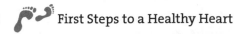

nicotine you take can be gradually reduced until you're off both cigarettes and nicotine.

- Medications like Zyban and Champix: These can be taken to reduce cravings and have been shown to prevent relapse back into smoking once the course is completed.
- Stop smoking clinics: The NHS in the UK offers support for people who want to quit. These may be held in your GP surgery or you can find out more by checking out the website www.nhs.uk/smokefree.

Monitoring your risk

Alongside these headline ways of maintaining a healthy heart by changing your lifestyle, you can also visit your GP practice to have a check up on your other risk factors for heart disease, like raised blood sugar and cholesterol, raised blood pressure, and signs of obesity.

Blood sugar

Diabetes is a condition which affects control of blood sugar. It has a wide range of possible complications throughout the body, including the circulation, where high levels of blood sugar can cause damage to blood vessel walls, accelerating the build-up of atheroma.

As a result it's important to check for this disease, which is done with a simple blood test at your GP surgery or clinic.

If you're diagnosed with diabetes you will need treatment, including changes to diet and some medication. The results may suggest that you are in an at-risk category for going on to develop diabetes in future and you may be advised to change your diet to try to stave it off.

Cholesterol

While cholesterol is the most well-known fat that we tend to monitor, there are other fats (lipids) in the blood that it's also a good idea to keep an eye on, such as triglycerides. Once again this can be done with a simple blood test, with a fasting sample being most accurate.

At high levels lipids can contribute to the build-up of atheroma in blood vessels, so if yours are found to be up you are likely to be given advice on how dietary changes and pills (statins) can help get the levels down.

Blood pressure

Persistently raised blood pressure can damage blood vessel walls and so it will need to be controlled. Full details of how this is done are found in Chapter 8.

Obesity

Obesity increases your risk of heart disease because it is associated with high blood lipid levels, an increased risk of diabetes, and, perhaps by default, reduced levels of exercise (people with a sedentary lifestyle tend to gain weight and then being overweight makes it more uncomfortable to engage in physical activity).

To find out if you are overweight or obese, your doctor or practice nurse will ask to measure your height and weight to calculate what's called your body mass index (BMI). This is a calculation which, in simple terms, determines whether you are the correct weight for your height. Having a low BMI, meaning you are grossly underweight, can be as bad for your health as having a raised BMI, which suggests you are obese.

They may also measure your waist circumference as this shows whether you are carrying too much weight around your middle.

First Steps to a Healthy Heart

If you are obese then you will be advised to lose weight. Your practice nurse may help with this but they may also advise that you access support from an organization like Weight Watchers or Slimming World, or from a dietitian.

Low carb diets

Diets that are low in carbohydrates have become increasingly popular over the past few years. Initially pioneered by American physician Dr Robert Atkins (no relation) in the 1970s, his Atkins Diet became so prominent that in 2002 he was named one of *TIME* magazine's Top 10 Persons of the Year.

Since his death in 2003 many similar diets have also taken off, each based on eating lower levels of carbohydrates, like bread, potatoes, and pasta, and instead relying on dietary fats and proteins, like meat, cheese, and avocados, as a source of energy. Avocados have become so popular that in 2017 prices rose dramatically when growers failed to keep up with demand.

Diabetes and low carb diets

The biggest benefits of following a low carb diet have been seen in people with diabetes. In this condition blood sugar levels are not adequately controlled by the hormone insulin and this, over time, causes damage to many of the body's tissues and organs.

In people with diabetes a low carb diet has been found to cause significant weight loss and many people who were diagnosed with Type 2 diabetes have even had their condition resolve, meaning they have become non-diabetic, without the use of medication. I've seen this in a number of patients in my own medical practice.

People with Type 1 diabetes have also found that following this type of diet improves their blood sugar control, making their condition much easier to manage.

Low carb vs low fat diets

There isn't, however, so far at least, any evidence to suggest that low carb diets are any better at helping people in the general population lose weight than more traditional low fat diets. And in 2018 when researchers from Stanford University Medical School in California published the results of a study that directly compared how much weight was lost by two groups of people each following one of these diets over a twelve-month period, they found almost identical levels of weight loss in both groups. Successful weight loss depended not on which diet was followed, but on how well people stuck to them.

Low carb diets and health

Another piece of research published in 2018, this time by doctors from Boston in the USA, suggested that low carb diets could actually be detrimental to health if the carbs were replaced by animal fats like meat, cheese, and butter. In contrast they found that those who substituted carbs for plant-based fats from avocados, nuts, and legumes (e.g. peas and lentils) were likely to live longer.

10
Living with heart disease

While heart disease is not curable it can, as we've seen in previous chapters, be managed with medicines, surgery, and a variety of lifestyle modifications. And the point of all of these measures – the pill popping, trips to the GP surgery or hospital, the operations, the exercise, healthier foods, and abstention from smoking etc. – is to have the best quality of life possible despite what's going on with your ticker.

So in this chapter we will take a look at how having a heart condition may limit certain activities and, most importantly, at some of the ways around the obstacles that can be presented.

Work

Being diagnosed with a heart condition, or even having had a heart attack or surgery, does not necessarily mean that you won't be able to work. But you may need to adapt what you do and how you do it, depending on your ongoing symptoms and the risk of further exacerbations of your particular condition. Your specialist and family doctor will be able to advise you about your particular situation by taking the following factors into consideration.

Your symptoms

As we've seen in earlier chapters, the most frequently experienced symptoms of the various types of heart disease are chest pain, shortness of breath, and palpitations (which can lead to episodes of fainting). Each of these can be made more likely to occur because of work-related activities, particularly those involving physical exertion, and each of them could pose a risk to the person experiencing them and to others because of the nature of the work being carried out, such as driving and operating heavy machinery.

Occupational hazards

Various hazards at work can either cause or make existing heart conditions worse. These can be physical, chemical, psychological, or ergonomic (due to the design of the workplace). The table below, based on a review article by Anne E. Price in the medical journal *Heart*, gives some examples.

Type of hazard	Potential risk
PHYSICAL	
Temperature	Extremes of heat or cold can affect blood flow to the heart.
Noise	Prolonged exposure to loud noise has been linked to a rise in blood pressure.
Patterns of exertion	Irregular but heavy exertion can increase the risk of heart attacks.

CHEMICAL	
Carbon monoxide	Exposure to high levels of this gas (e.g. when working on diesel engines) reduces oxygen supply to the heart and can trigger angina, heart attacks, and arrhythmias.
Solvents (e.g. those used in chemical manufacture, dry cleaning, glue, and paint)	A small number of solvents have been linked to heart arrhythmias.
PSYCHOSOCIAL	
Job stress	Research has shown that high levels of job stress can raise blood pressure and cause an increased risk of developing cardiovascular disease.
Shift work (e.g. shift patterns involving switching between day and night work)	There is evidence that this increases risk of cardiovascular disease too (this may be due to disruption of the body's normal circadian rhythms and a person's eating patterns).

Personal factors

It's not only the nature of the work or workplace that will affect someone's ability to carry on or return to their job; a number of personal factors will also come into play. These will include age of the person and number of years left until retirement, suitability (and willingness) to be redeployed or retrained to do something new, the level of fulfilment found doing the particular job, the attitude of employers towards illness and the likelihood of them supporting an employee's decision to continue working with a serious health condition.

People may also be reluctant to return to work because they had their heart attack while they were at work, because of a more general fear that they will put themselves at risk of further illness if they don't take it easy from now on, and even because they will get more money from disability benefits than they would from carrying on with their previous job.

Effects of medicines

Any medicine can give us side effects and each of us has different susceptibilities to them. It's therefore important when starting potentially long-term new treatments for your heart that you discuss the possible side effects of your particular drug with your doctor or pharmacist to make sure they are unlikely to affect you at work.

Sex

While people will often ask about how heart disease may affect many aspects of their lives I often find, especially working in British general practice, that most people won't directly ask me about how their sex lives might be affected by a new diagnosis of heart disease. It's a bit like the classic comedy sketch of the teenage lad going into the pharmacy to ask for condoms but losing his nerve and coming out with a comb, a toothbrush, and a deodorant instead.

So to save the anxiety of asking the question I'll just come out and say it: you don't have to stop having sex if you have heart disease. You might have to take it a bit easier, but it's certainly not off limits.

A few tips

Any physical activity can of course be genuinely anxiety provoking when you have a heart condition. And when it comes to more intimate moments there's obviously the fear that you'll get symptoms and spoil things for your partner. Or that you won't be able to perform as you used to.

So these tips are aimed at trying to prevent this normally enjoyable part of life from becoming a cause of stress.

First, the general advice is to hold off on sexual activity for four to six weeks after having a heart attack or heart surgery.

Secondly, make it a pleasant experience to lower anxiety, maybe starting with touching and kissing rather than getting too physical too soon.

Finally, be sensible. Don't have sex on a full stomach or when you've had a fair amount to drink. Ask your partner to be more active if you think you'll struggle and, of course, if you have angina keep your spray nearby in case you get any chest pain.

Sexual problems

It's quite common after being diagnosed with a serious illness or after having had a heart attack to lose interest in sex for a while. Men can also show signs of erectile dysfunction, again due to anxiety, but also because of the side effects of some of the medicines used to treat heart disease.

Often these issues will settle with time as couples build up confidence in being intimate with each other. If not, there's plenty that doctors and specialist nurses can do, so please don't be afraid to ask.

Holidays

Research published in the summer of 2018 by a group of Finnish researchers suggested that all GPs should prescribe holidays for people at risk of heart disease because having a decent length holiday was shown to be beneficial. Sadly, that's not possible in the UK's cash-strapped National Health Service. And what about holidays for people who already have established heart disease? Is that such a good idea?

The good news is that if you feel well and your condition is well controlled then you should be fine to go. You could obviously run the idea by your doctor first, but sadly they still won't be able to prescribe it for you.

When planning a holiday there are a few important factors

to take into consideration alongside the usual advice about wearing sunscreen, getting the appropriate vaccinations, and not drinking the water in some of the world's more far-flung places.

- Make sure you have enough medication with you to last throughout the holiday and carry an up-to-date list of all your pills in case you run into trouble while you're away and need to seek medical help.
- Pick accommodation near all the attractions and local amenities so you don't have too much exertion and hassle getting around.
- Avoid destinations that are either very hot or very cold and those that are situated at high altitude, as your heart could be affected by both extremes of temperature and lower oxygen levels.
- If you're planning a trip abroad then check with your GP or specialist about your fitness to fly. As long as your condition is stable you should be fine.
- If you have a pacemaker or internal defibrillator, make sure you take its identification card with you. Devices should be absolutely fine going through all airport scanners but it's better to be safe rather than sorry and have the product details with you in case you need to double check.
- Make sure you have adequate insurance, owning up to – and therefore having cover – for all your medical conditions. Being hospitalized abroad will be a very expensive business – especially in the United States where it can cost at least $3,000 for a trip to the emergency room. So even if you've not had a heart attack, you probably will if you're uninsured when they present you with the bill.

Appendix: Further sources of advice and information

Having looked at some of the first steps to having a healthy heart you may want to find out more. In this section, I've listed some of the organizations from around the world that provide help and support on a variety of heart-related topics.

United Kingdom

British Heart Foundation
They are involved in funding research and campaigning for people affected by heart disease. Their website is also full of invaluable information.
www.bhf.org.uk

British Society for Heart Failure
Their aim is to increase knowledge among health professionals and promote research into all aspects of heart failure and to provide expert advice to patients, professionals, and the NHS.
www.bsh.org.uk

Cardiomyopathy UK
They provide help, support, and advice on all aspects of heart muscle disease.
www.cardiomyopathy.org

NHS
This website contains information about all aspects of health and disease, including pages on heart disease.
www.nhs.uk

Australia

The Heart Foundation
This organization funds research into heart disease and its prevention, and its website is a very useful source of information on all aspects of diseases which affect the heart.
www.heartfoundation.org.au

Healthdirect
Much like the NHS website in the UK, this site covers all aspects of health, including heart disease.
www.healthdirect.gov.au

Canada

Cardiac Health Foundation of Canada
They are a charity dedicated to keeping Canadians' hearts healthy, focusing on cardiac rehabilitation as well as advocacy for disease prevention and education.
www.cardiachealth.ca

Heart and Stroke
This organization supports research into the treatment of both heart disease and stroke, and their prevention. Their website is also a great source of information and advice.
www.heartandstroke.ca

New Zealand

Heart Foundation
Their mission is to "stop all people in New Zealand dying prematurely from heart disease and enable people with heart disease to live full lives" and their website is full of advice about how to try and do just that.
www.heartfoundation.org.nz

Ministry of Health NZ
This is the New Zealand government's site for advice on all aspects of health and disease, including heart disease.
www.health.govt.nz

United States

American Heart Association
As well as funding research and developing public health programmes, they have a great website full of advice and information for both the public and healthcare professionals.
www.heart.org

The Heart Foundation
This charitable organization has been set up in memory of Steven S. Cohen, who died of a heart attack when he was only thirty-five years old. It funds research and provides advice about how to keep your own heart healthy.
www.theheartfoundation.org